"What a valuable resource! Every woman needs a friend who will read this book and agree to pray for each other's marriages. Every church and every neighborhood needs a Praying Wives Club!"

—PAM FARREL
Author, *Men Are Like Waffles, Women Are Like Spaghetti* and
10 Best Decisions a Woman Can Make

"What a timely book affirming the camaraderie of women and the power of Scripture! Marita and Dianne invite readers into their lives as they share personal struggles and thought-provoking prayers that can heal hurts and transform hearts."

—KARI WEST
Conference speaker and author, *When He Leaves:*
Help and Hope for Hurting Wives

"In an age where society conspires to undermine marriage, *The Praying Wives Club* gives us a practical, doable way to strengthen our marriages. Their emphasis on upholding and supporting our husbands is refreshing and encouraging. I love the addition of specific prayers that make it easy for anyone, experienced prayer or novice, to experience the power of prayer. Whether you are a newlywed or an old-timer like me (48 years), praying for your husband will refresh and renew your love for him and the Lord."

—BETTY SOUTHARD
Speaker and author, *The Grandmother Book,*
Come As You Are, and *The Mentor Quest*

"What a wonderful, practical, and potentially life-changing book! While many clubs are merely cliques with fancy names, a Praying Wives Club tackles real issues in the lives of real people. I highly recommend both the book and the concept to any wife regardless of age or length of marriage."

—GAYLE ROPER
Author, *Allah's Fire*

"Marita and Dianne live what they write. With welcome honesty they share how their girlfriend gatherings turned into God-honoring meetings to pray for their mates, and the impact goes far beyond relationships. It motivated me to stop whining and start working on a Praying Wives Club. Full of practical tips, this book will inspire every wife who prays for her man."

—JAN COLEMAN
Speaker and author of *The Woman Behind the Mask*

"Authors Marita Littauer and Dianne Anderson have put together the most practical marriage manual on the market today. Every woman who is now, ever has been, or ever plans to be a wife needs to read this book— and put its principles into practice."

—KATHI MACIAS
Speaker and author of 16 books, including the popular Matthews & Matthews Detective series

"Ever had a disagreement with your husband? Does his situation with a job, the children, or his health cause you concern? Then you'll love *The Praying Wives Club!* Marita Littauer and Dianne Anderson make themselves vulnerable as they give advice from their experience with their own husbands and their friends who pray for them. This practical book gives you all you need to begin and maintain a Praying Wives Club. You'll find tools to help you establish a vital, growing group of prayer warriors surrounding and supporting your marriage."

—EDNA ELLISON, Ph.D.
Christian mentoring guru, author of the *Friend to Friend* Bible study series

"Marita Littauer and Dianne Anderson formed the Praying Wives Club as an emotional support group to pray for their husbands and their marriages. . . . Their success has led them to write this book to show other women how to start a Praying Wives Club, where they, too, can bear one another's burdens in confidence."

—SUSAN TITUS OSBORN
Speaker and author of 28 books including the Parable in Action series and *Rest Stops for Busy Moms*

The Praying Wives Club

Gather Your Girlfriends
and Pray for Your Marriage

The Praying Club Wives

Marita Littauer & Dianne Anderson

Kregel
Publications

The Praying Wives Club: Gather Your Girlfriends and Pray for Your Marriage

© 2006 by Marita Littauer and Dianne Anderson

Published by Kregel Publications, a division of Kregel, Inc., P.O. Box 2607, Grand Rapids, MI 49501.

ISBN 0-8254-3150-6

Printed in the United States of America

06 07 08 09 10 / 5 4 3 2 1

Contents

Every Marriage Needs Prayer

"Help! My marriage is in trouble." Most of us have said that at one time or another. Maybe you're saying it right now. Regardless of where your marriage relationship is today—somewhere between terrible and terrific—chances are it could be better . . . and prayer will help. If you'd like to see improvement in your marriage, in your husband, and in your attitude, this book is for you.

Several years ago, a friend asked if I'd like to get together once a week with a couple of other wives to pray for our husbands and our marriages. Though I thought my marriage was pretty good— better than most—I, like many women, knew my marriage could use improvement. So I agreed.

Four of us started meeting together. Three of us stayed with it for several years. Our marriages were in different stages, and during those years, we supported, encouraged, and prayed for one another through many difficult times. While sweeping change was not apparent in each woman's marriage at any given time, we discovered that at the very least, praying for our marriages brought about changes in our attitudes. Each marriage experienced improvement, and we saw many difficulties overcome by miraculous resolutions.

We eventually called our weekly gatherings "The Praying Wives Club." In the morning, before leaving the house, I'd tell my husband, "The Praying Wives Club is meeting today. Is there anything specific you want us to pray for?" Sometimes he had a request, other times he didn't. But he knew and appreciated our positive and proactive approach.

After a few years of praying together, the stresses in our collective marriages seemed to settle. Our schedules grew more complicated, and our weekly meetings were disbanded—though not forgotten. When I began this book, it had been a couple of years since I'd gathered with a group of girlfriends for purposeful prayer about our husbands and our marriages. For most of that period, I'd also enjoyed marital stability.

As I shared stories of our little prayer group with other women around the country, it became obvious that many women longed for a marital safety net like I was describing. I began to sense, too, a growing need on my own part to be in another Praying Wives Club. My husband, Chuck, and I had recently moved from the temporary house we had purchased ten years earlier—we intended to live in it for only about two years while we looked for the "right" house. While I was ecstatic to finally be moving, finances necessitated that the dream home we could afford was one that was incomplete and needed a lot of work. By default, I became the general contractor—something in which I had no experience. We lived through the construction and moved in. Now we were living in the house of our dreams, something neither of us ever thought we could afford, and yet our lives were not paradise. There was an underlying tension.

As I prayed about our lack of marital bliss, God pointed out to me that we were in a place of transition, that our marital equilibrium had been upset by the move. I called Dianne and suggested we resurrect the Praying Wives Club. Her marriage, too, was in a place of transition. Another friend also needed to be part of a Praying Wives Club. Her marital equilibrium was off balance because of her recent reentry into the workforce. The three of us agreed to gather together in a new Praying Wives Club. When word got out among friends and acquaintances, two others asked to join us. Our new group's formation concurred with the writing of this book, so we all agreed to be guinea pigs for the guidance this book would provide.

In addition, a large group of women who live all across the country have participated via e-mail in the creation of this book. Some started their own groups, using material from this book as a guide, and have shared their experiences with me. Others read the draft and told stories of their own prayer experiences so I could include them in the book for you.

Because I'm the writer, when you see the pronoun "I," it will refer to me, Marita Littauer. Dianne's contributions will refer to her as Dianne, not "I" unless otherwise noted—such as in her personal story on the following pages. (Due to her visibility in the community and her more private personality, our third friend—whose idea it was to form the first Praying Wives Club—has asked to remain anonymous.) Others who have shared stories will be referred to by their first names.

On the following pages, Dianne and I tell our own stories, as well as the stories of other women who belong to a Praying Wives Club.

As you read about the work that God is doing in our marriages as we continue to pray, you'll surely want the same type of results for your marriage. We hope, then, that you'll be inspired to gather your girlfriends and pray specifically for your marriage! As you read about the pattern used to form our group, you'll be equipped to gather your girlfriends and create your own Praying Wives Club.

The combination of my firm belief in the power of prayer and the virtually universal need to improve and protect marriages has resulted in this book. Your marriage may be in a better—or worse—condition than ours, and your needs may be different and unique to your situation. But we trust that seeing our process of growth will motivate you to gather your girlfriends and pray for your marriage!

Acknowledgments

Special thanks to all the women who served as readers through our e-mail reading group. We hope that your participation in the creation of this book was at least half as helpful to you as it was to us.

We also thank Becky for allowing her Praying Wives Club to be our "guinea pig" group. Thank you for offering us feedback and sharing your successes with the world.

To our own Praying Wives Club and our husbands, thank you for your love, support, and feedback during the writing of this book. But mostly, thank you for allowing us to share your lives with the world, so that through our experiences many marriages may be enriched, perhaps even saved.

Section 1

WHAT DOES A PRAYING WIVES CLUB LOOK LIKE?

Chapter 1

Marita's Story

Several years ago, I was at a point where, in our nearly twenty years of union, our marriage had weathered its share of storms, yet had anyone asked, I would have said it was better than most. Despite the dips we'd had, we actually still liked each other, did fun things, and had a good sex life.

Chuck and I met when mutual friends set us up. His best friend and my best friend lived in the same complex of condominiums. His friend had seen me drive up to my friend's place in a British sports car. It was a beautiful fall day in California and I had the top down on my TR7 and was wearing short shorts. Based on two features—my car and my legs—Chuck's friend talked to my friend and they arranged for us to meet. While it wasn't love at first sight, it did take place pretty quickly. My friends all knew Chuck must be "it" when I went out with him more than three times. He was the opposite of everything I seemed attracted to. I was basically dating for a good time and jewelry acquisition. I was not looking for a husband. I was twenty-four. I dated older, well-off men. Chuck was twenty-seven and in the Air Force. He was newly single, after a brief marriage. He had nothing but an old Jaguar, and he was renting a room from his boss. Even so, he was very handsome, his military uniform accented his slim build, and his low-key personality seemed to beg me to cheer him up. I did. We got married five months after we met.

In our first year of marriage, Chuck left the Air Force to pursue a career in motion-picture production in Hollywood. We lived there for a year and discovered that the film industry is all about who you know, not what you know. Chuck's degree in motion picture production from a prestigious school meant little to the self-made men in Hollywood. After a year of struggle—and debt acquisition—we moved back to San Bernardino, where Chuck went to work in the same building where he'd worked the year before, only now as a contract worker making movies for the military.

We spent a few hard years there until an inheritance gave Chuck the freedom to try out his dream. We moved to San Diego's North County, where Chuck opened a photography studio. Within a year, finances determined that dream's death. Fortunately, Chuck still had some of his inheritance and was able to go back to school and get a master's degree in psychology. Meanwhile, he did training films for the San Diego Police Department. Chuck graduated with plans of a career as a marriage therapist. Unfortunately, it was the exact time (to the day, it seemed) that insurance companies quit paying for people to get counseling. Chuck is a Republican, NRA member, Rush Limbaugh-listening Christian, but the only job he could find was as a social worker for the County of San Diego. His conservative views on life and the liberal leanings of social work made for an uncomfortable fit.

In the midst of Chuck's search for satisfying and stable work, we did manage to purchase a starter home in Carlsbad, California, and later were able to move up to a lovely executive-type house.

After a couple of years in social work, attempting to glean the hours needed to get his marriage and family counseling license in California, Chuck added up his "supervised" hours. He discovered that there was no way he could get the required hours by the deadline. He applied for jobs in states that would recognize his education and experience but that had not yet required licensure. Right away he got a job in New Mexico. His new employer wanted him, in fact, to start in two weeks.

I stayed in our brand-new, upscale home in Carlsbad, California, while Chuck lived in a two-bedroom, one-bath bungalow built in the 1940s (with few updated features) in Carlsbad, New Mexico. I joined him when I could, and when I eventually found renters for our California house, I moved to New Mexico full time. If you've ever been to Carlsbad, California—in San Diego's North County—and to Carlsbad, New Mexico, you can understand my culture shock. Carlsbad, California, is a coastal community north of San Diego and is home to the famous La Costa Golf Resort and Spa. Carlsbad, New Mexico, is a small mining town located all by itself in the southeastern corner of New Mexico and is best known for the Carlsbad Caverns—though these days most of the economic growth and news coverage comes from storing nuclear waste. It felt like the time we spent in Carlsbad, New Mexico, was a long year. Though, during that time, Chuck was able to qualify for the newly instated licensing in the state—making him more marketable. After a year in Carlsbad, Chuck was offered a position as the marriage therapist for the Minirth-Meier Clinic in Albuquerque—back when there was a Minirth-Meier Clinic and their business was booming. We jumped at the chance and, within two weeks, moved to Albuquerque.

Seven years later, when we were settled in Albuquerque, changes in the mental-health field unsettled his employment. After unsuccessfully applying for jobs at Home Depot and the like, he finally found a job in Colorado at a residential treatment center. Remembering the last time we were forced to live apart, I cried and fussed over his decision and, finally, marriage counseling was needed for me to change my position and okay his move. I stayed in our basic tract house, while Chuck rented a one-bedroom apartment in Colorado Springs. Neither of our separations was due to marital problems, but you can be sure both *caused* problems.

In contrast to Chuck's career path, my course has been so stable, it's nearly boring. I was a Christian speaker and writer when we met, and twenty-two years later, I still am. I have been the primary breadwinner most of our married life. Because my employment doesn't require that I live in any one specific place, it's remained steady. However, several of our moves to accommodate Chuck's work have uprooted me from friends, family, and office.

Not only were jobs, houses, and moves a stress on our marriage, but Chuck and I also have opposite personality types. I am what is called a Popular Sanguine (see "Personality Overviews" in Appendix C). One of the key traits of my personality is that I have no secrets. Chuck is a Perfect Melancholy, for whom privacy is very important. I want to give everyone who enters our home a house tour—even when the house is not one with which I'm enamoured. In our previous house, I especially liked to show people the garage, as most people's jaws dropped at the sight of the neatly organized collection of vehicles we had jammed into our two-car garage. (In the front row were all the left-leaning motorcycles, the back row, all those that lean right. Plus there was a Jaguar and several bicycles.) Chuck had the garage alarmed and had rigged up a dead-bolt system with a steel rod going into the concrete to prevent break-ins. The door from the house to the garage required a key. If someone broke into the house, they could not get into the garage. It was a different key from the front door. If we had a house-/dog-sitter, they didn't have a key to the garage. All those locks wore me out, and I was constantly in trouble for not being security-conscious enough.

With the circuitous route we took to the present, children never fit into the picture. We always thought, *Maybe next year we'll be in a better place.* We never were. (After twenty-two years of marriage, we've never had children—and we know now that we never will.

By that point, though, we'd lived through a lot and still liked each other most of the time. I would have said we were happily married. Yet when a newlywed friend suggested we get together once a week to pray for our marriages, I was interested. While we had reached a somewhat settled place, I was eager to pray for my husband. When our group began to pray, Chuck had recently returned to New Mexico—we were now living together again—following his five months in Colorado with me driving back and forth between the two states on weekends. He was a licensed mental health counselor in two states, but he was selling cars—albeit Jaguars. There's nothing wrong with selling cars, but it doesn't require a master's degree, and it was never Chuck's career choice. For me, I loved having a different Jaguar in the driveway all the time, and Chuck has been a collector of Jaguars for as long as I have known him. In fact, we have one (it's thirty-five years old and doesn't run) in the garage now—and a few were sacrificed during our various times of economic uncertainty. But Chuck was unhappy with his life, which made me unhappy.

I kept dreaming of a house I could love, even be proud of. Every time I'd find a house that I thought suited us better than the house where we lived, Chuck would refuse to even look at it. He hated New Mexico. We still owned the little house in Carlsbad (NM). He didn't want any more real estate here. He was unwilling to buy a house in New Mexico that was anything but the basic house because our needs were unusual—few bedrooms and lots of garage space—and therefore would be hard to sell. He kept hoping that God would allow him to leave this forsaken land.

The problem was, we didn't fit into the house we lived in. We had too much furniture, as our house in California was considerably larger, and since we'd moved to New Mexico my parents had moved and given us numerous pieces. I didn't want to part with any of it, as I was sure we'd have a bigger house soon. During the years we'd lived in New Mexico, Chuck had acquired a quantity of old cars and motorcycles (remember, we don't have children), which made it nearly impossible even to walk through the garage, let alone park the vehicles we drove. Every time he was frustrated with our cramped quarters and declared that we needed to move, I'd have a spark of hope and go house hunting. I'd find a few that might work and come home with pictures. By then, Chuck was back in his not-buying-more-real-estate-in-New-Mexico mode.

So when we wives began to gather, I had been on an emotional roller-coaster. Chuck was depressed. We'd been married nearly twenty years, had worked out most—but, obviously, not all—of our difficulties, and were committed to staying married.

For two years the praying wives met almost every week. Each of us had varied and over-full schedules, but each week we'd get out our calendars and find the next date that worked. We made prayer a priority.

As we shared our hearts with each other and committed to pray, we began to see changes—often in our own attitudes. For me, the biggest miracle was Chuck's employment. When Chuck returned to New Mexico after five months in Colorado, he had a couple of short jobs (the kind you do not put on a résumé). He landed at Melloy Jaguar in Albuquerque, and felt that God told him to be content there. Chuck stayed there for almost two years, during which time he told God, "If You want me to have a different job, You are going to have to make that very clear." Chuck was not going looking; he no longer spent a good portion of his Sunday scanning the classifieds.

They liked Chuck at the Jaguar dealership, and in no time he was the senior salesman, and making good money. While the job was not intellectually rewarding, it was low stress. During the freezing weather of winter or the dust storms of spring, not many people wanted to shop for cars. As a result, Chuck was frequently the only one in the dealership, giving him lots of time to sit at a desk and wait for customers to come in. During this downtime, he read his Bible from cover to cover—something he had never done before. He and I also wrote our first book together. Chuck is a Licensed Professional Clinical Counselor (LPCC) whose specialty is marriage, so our book was on . . . marriage.

Still, he was restless. The Praying Wives Club prayed for a better job for Chuck, the right job for his skills and education and one that was intellectually stimulating. One day, while Chuck was sitting at his desk in the Jaguar dealership, a man and woman came in. They hadn't come to buy a car. Chuck knew the man, a psychiatrist he had worked with at the Minirth-Meier Clinic. The man and woman were colleagues at one of the largest providers of health care in the state, and they offered Chuck a job in upper management.

That launched Chuck back into the field of mental health. He no longer works for that company, but he's still in mental health care management, maintains a small private practice, is well-known throughout the state, and is respected in his field. He's frequently offered jobs, and his income—which is more than mine—has been stable ever since.

While God truly answered our prayers about Chuck's job, He also blessed me with a house I love. It's my dream house! Plus, the two-year, one-month, and eleven-day miracle of acquiring this house has convinced Chuck that God wants us in New Mexico, and now he has a good attitude about this state that he often referred to as a "third-world country!"

However, the process of buying this incomplete house, having the construction done to make it livable, and finally moving into it has presented us with a new set of challenges. It has unsettled the equilibrium we had previously established and has put us into a place of transition. Help! I know prayer works. I need to gather my girlfriends and pray for my marriage—again!

Chapter 2

Dianne's Story

All my married life, I'd prayed for my husband. Usually the prayers were quick little arrows shot upward: "Protect him, Lord," or "Help him in this situation," or even "Show him that I'm right and he's wrong." But when offered the chance to get together with friends on a regular basis for deeper, more purposeful prayer for our husbands, I thought, *Why not!*

At the time, Mark and I had been married for nine years and had a strong, healthy relationship. Before we knew each other, we'd both spent our twenties focusing on careers in television news—a demanding, all-consuming business that left little time for socializing. We met on the job at our TV station, and our courtship was quick. We were engaged after five months and married two months after that. Since I was already in my early thirties, we went right to work on a family. Our son was born a little more than a year later and our daughter arrived twenty months after that. Even with so much, so soon, we settled into a committed, comfortable relationship.

We had the typical trials of getting used to living with another person after being on our own for many years. Our biggest challenges came, though, when Mark left TV news. Our son wasn't quite a year old when we finally accepted that it was too hard to raise a child with both parents working for the same station. We both worked until 11 P.M. three nights a week, forcing us to leave the baby with a neighborhood sitter late into the night. I had the higher profile position as a news anchor, and consequently the higher salary, so Mark decided to quit his job as a reporter and start his own business. He was excited about the opportunity to get out of TV and into a profession that he could control better and that would reward him for his hard work.

As though our lives were not hectic enough—balancing two careers and two babies—we complicated things even more when we built our dream home in a village on the outskirts of Albuquerque. We had visions of an adobe-accented Southwestern home with a large horse pasture, surrounded by rose bushes. And that's what we got—along with the hours of work required to maintain the property. It left little money and even less time to play. Mark had begun to work out of a home office and found himself constantly distracted from his media-consulting business. The house- and horse-related chores never seemed to end. After a few years of constant stress and pressure, his health began to fail.

Mark first contracted viral meningitis in the early summer of our seventh year of marriage. It took more than a week for doctors to figure out what was causing his symptoms—the debilitating headache and light sensitivity that left him incapable of anything other than lying in bed in a darkened room. He had barely recovered from this first bout when he was hit again two months later. This time he spent several days in the hospital on a morphine drip to relieve some of the pounding pain caused by the swelling in his brain. Since it was viral—not bacterial—the doctors could only treat him with painkillers.

But the most difficult time came afterward, when the headaches lingered. Fighting to regain some control of his life, Mark turned inward as he tried to cope with the constant pain. He became withdrawn, silent, moody. Never having struggled with health problems, and seeing no obvious, outward signs of sickness, I soon lost my patience. My lack of sympathy and growing irritation sent Mark even deeper into himself. Our wedding vows said "in sickness and in health," but I hadn't grasped the impact that a long-term illness can have on a relationship.

It was in the midst of our struggle that we realized our rush to have everything we'd ever wanted—kids, house, careers, horses—had left us no time to enjoy any of it. We were victims of our own success. We needed to regain control of our lives, and downsizing was our only option. We sold our dream house and moved closer to my work, our church, and the kids' school. It was a difficult decision because we'd poured everything we had into that home—our money, our time, our hearts. Yet it had robbed us of Mark's health and our happiness. The change to a different home was drastic, but the results were dramatic.

We found a smaller, less-expensive house, more centrally located, that required minimal upkeep. Feeling a sense of relief, Mark began working out of our home office, writing a book to promote his business. He spent months researching, analyzing, organizing, writing, and rewriting. At the same time, he still battled with chronic headaches and daily fatigue. Many afternoons, he wanted only to lie down for a nap, but he pushed himself to keep going. At times the struggle made him feel depressed, which made his headaches and fatigue worse.

After we settled into our new house, I took up running and he soon followed. The physical exertion became an outlet to relieve stress, and his headaches diminished, although they didn't go away. Slowly, he seemed to regain a passion for his work. I relaxed a little, finding it easier to balance home, kids, and work in these new surroundings. Everything now appeared more calm and in control on the surface. Yet, hidden beneath, was the reminder of how quickly it could all come apart again. Every time Mark came under increased stress, his headaches worsened, and both of us held our breaths, hoping and praying we wouldn't have to go through that painful trial again.

It was at this point that Marita and another friend suggested getting together to pray. Seeing the opportunity to do something proactive to keep our marriage on the right track, I quickly agreed. We met for just an hour or so every few weeks, and I began to see changes. The first change was in my attitude toward Mark's health problems. Then it was in actual changes in our lives. We praying wives chalked up a big answer to prayer when Mark finished his book and landed a publisher within weeks, a process that can take months, years, or may never happen at all. But the most memorable moment came when he called on my cell phone while the three of us wives were meeting. His online book sales rating, he said, was shooting up with no obvious explanation. Later in the day, we found out his book had been reviewed in the prestigious *Wall Street Journal.* His book never, in fact, got a bad review, which is interesting, because we'd braced ourselves and prayed that a bad review wouldn't discourage him.

The book's success led the way for Mark to move into an executive office. There he could be away from his homebound workspace full of distractions by kids, phones, pets, and neighbors. His business and his confidence grew steadily. While the praying wives can take no real credit—all that work is God's grace alone—it brought us pleasure to see our request not only answered but answered abundantly, far beyond our expectations. Why are we surprised when God does exactly what He promises He'll do?

Months later, my husband sent a heartfelt note to my prayer partners, thanking them for their quiet, persistent, devoted talks with God on his behalf. Coming from a guy who doesn't easily or readily express his feelings, that note was a true testament to the power of purposeful prayer.

Section 2

WHY SHOULD I START A PRAYING WIVES CLUB?

Chapter 3

Support

A person standing alone can be attacked and defeated, but two can stand back-to-back and conquer. Three are even better, for a triple-braided cord is not easily broken.

—Ecclesiastes 4:12 NLT

Are you thinking by now that a Praying Wives Club sounds like a good idea? Praying is, of course, always a good idea. But if you create your own group and it continues to meet in prayer, you'll discover the great benefit provided by the support system in a Praying Wives Club. This small group of women will come to know more about you than your other friends do—more, perhaps, than even your family does. As you share together, you begin to understand, as no on else can, what you're each facing.

Sometimes the support comes in the form of practical help, sometimes it's a hug, and at other times the Praying Wives Club acts as a first-response team.

When Dianne's husband, Mark, was still working at home and the kids were out of school for the summer, it created a climate ripe for conflict. His home office was located right next to the

living room, with the front door on one side and the kids' bedrooms on the other. He was trying to concentrate while writing
on the computer, or trying to be professional while talking with
clients on the phone. The kids, on the other hand, were being
kids. They wanted Popsicles. They wanted their friends to come
over. They played the TV too loudly. They fought. All the com-
motion was a constant strain and stress for their dad. Dianne started
work at two in the afternoon, so she was home most of the day.
Mark wanted her to keep the children quiet—which was, of course,
impossible. He was unhappy with her for not keeping the kids
under control. She was unhappy that he expected her to. Dianne
felt bad both for the kids and her husband. The kids needed a
place to play, and he needed a place to work. We prayed about it
in our group.

As so happened, our third Praying Wives Club member was in
real estate. She knew of a building near Dianne's house that had
nice executive suites at an affordable price. As an added bonus,
many of the men who had offices in the suite were Christians. She
suggested the solution to Dianne, who went home and discussed
it with Mark. They checked out the property, and it worked. Within
a week, Mark had moved his office out of the house and into his
own quiet space where he had a built-in support system of godly
men. Once working in his new office, Mark realized he'd missed
working around other people. He enjoyed making new friends and
talking with them on a daily basis. He even developed a close
friendship with another guy in the office complex with whom he
could bounce around ideas or go to lunch. The move required
some afternoon child care, but the improvement in Mark's produc-
tivity and in their marriage more than made up for the additional
cost.

Another time, Dianne and Mark's anniversary was approaching
and they had no family in the area who could take the kids overnight to allow them time alone. As with the office solution, this

was an easy fix. I took the kids overnight. Before we connected to hand off the children, Dianne called me to ask if I had any appropriate attire that she could borrow for their night of romantic intimacy. I have a wardrobe of "little black somethings," and I brought her a few selections. From that point on, about once a month I try to take the kids overnight to give Dianne and Mark time alone. However, Chuck thinks my lingerie wardrobe—all gifts from him— should remain private.

Back when my marriage was in a rough phase, Dianne and I developed a sort of code. I'm not a morning coffee drinker. When I do drink coffee, I like high-end café mocha. It's my choice for comfort food. My natural inclination for a mocha is around 10:30 A.M. and 3:00 P.M. So if I call Dianne at 9:00 A.M. and say, "I am at Starbucks!" nothing more needs to be said. She knows I've had a tough morning and need some "poor-babies." Sometimes we meet for a "Starbucks moment" and exchange poor-babies in person.

Through the Praying Wives Club we developed what we affectionately refer to as "The Poor Baby Network." Sometimes it helps just to have someone who understands and cares and simply says, "poor baby, poor baby." The women in our group were perfect for this type of empathy, because we had a deeper understanding of one another's marriages and situations. It was a safe place to spout off, knowing that our frustrations would be taken in context and in confidence. Also, because we all knew our commitment to our marriages was even more solid than our friendship, sometimes we'd come to the defense of the other's husband, saying, "You know he didn't mean it that way," or "Just give him some space; it'll be okay."

Because the praying wives network is composed of women, we respond to anxiety in pretty much the same way. Men, in general, want to fix things, while women are better at simply giving a hug— even if it's only figuratively. Both Dianne and I have a penchant for getting overbooked. There are just so many things we want to do! Most of the time we do well with over-packed schedules, and eventually we get it all done. But some days we crack. It usually happens when our husbands ask us to do one more thing. We bark back with something like, "Can you not see I'm pedaling as fast as I can? I *can't* do one more thing today!"

Chuck is a therapist so he typically rolls with the flow of the chaos created by a harried wife's schedule. Mark is more pragmatic. He responds by reminding Dianne that "somebody always pays." What he means is that there's only so much one person can do. When Dianne takes on more than she can handle, her family gets the short end of the deal, and her grumpiness usually compounds the problem. Mark feels Dianne should fix what causes her anxiety in the first place, emphasizing that he's told her not to say "Yes" so often. It's up to her to pare down her life to a manageable capacity.

How nice it is at times of stress to have a friend to call who will simply allow you to vent your frustrations and offer "poor-baby" verbal hugs, but not beat up on your husband for being mean or not understanding. The Praying Wives Club can offer such support.

Pam's recent call is a different example of benefits of the Praying Wives network. Pam is in our new Praying Wives Club, and as a pastor's wife, she's grateful to have a group outside of her church with whom she can be honest. One Wednesday evening she called me. We'd been friends and colleagues before the Praying Wives Club, so when I saw her name on the caller ID, I answered with a chirpy, "Hello, hello, hello!" As soon as Pam responded, I knew "chirpy" was not the right tone.

Through tears, Pam explained that she was terrified. She was calling me from the church parking lot. Her teenage son, who is from a previous marriage, had made a very poor choice—typical of teenagers. Before their church prayer meeting, her husband, David, had gone to pick up her son from a sports practice. Her son was not there and was reported not to have shown up all week. He appeared before too long and was unharmed. The crowd he was with, however, and their known behaviors were cause for great alarm. Pam was concerned that David would lash out in anger at her son. While David has never been physically abusive, her first husband was—which caused her residual fear in the current situation.

She called me while David was still in church for the prayer meeting. Her son was in the car, and she was in the parking lot. As she tearfully relayed the incident, she asked that I pray for her, her son, and her husband, and that her husband would handle the difficulty reasonably—without hurting her son. I promised I would and offered to call the other Praying Wives. I dialed each of them and shared Pam's dilemma. We all committed to stop right then and pray, and to continue to pray for the situation.

At the Praying Wives Club meeting just a few days earlier, Pam chose an interesting Scripture prayer. The one she had selected to pray for her husband that week—and each agreed to pray for her as well—was prayer F.6 from the Parenting section (see appendix A). That prayer is based on Colossians 3:21: "Help [David] to discipline in love and not in anger. Help him to be constructive in his corrections so that he will not crush the children's spirits, but will shape them into the godly young people You desire them to be." As we prayed in response to her 911 prayer request, we also prayed her chosen Scripture prayer.

We connected by phone the next day. Our prayers had been answered. David had been reasonable in his disciplining of his stepson. Pam's son was in big trouble and his boundaries had been tightened—but he was physically unharmed. At our next gathering, Pam told us how much support she felt from knowing that we were praying for her. We rejoiced together in the answered prayer, knowing that any one of us could be the next one to need the support of our Praying Wives Club.

Not every situation, of course, is assured a happy ending. But being a part of a Praying Wives Club can assure a much-needed support system that's hard to come by in today's transient society.

Chapter 4

Success

It is not that we think we can do anything of lasting value by ourselves. Our only power and success come from God.

—2 Corinthians 3:5 NLT

In both of the Praying Wives Clubs I've been part of, we've had great successes as a result of our cooperative prayers. During a recent workshop, for example, I hoped to have the attendees come and see my dream house. Remember how Chuck values privacy? My Praying Wives Club prayed about that. Success! Chuck agreed they could come. About twenty chatty ladies arrived on our doorstep. He was home and was charming to them. I toured them all through the house—expect for his spaces. For my close friends who'd arrived from across the country, he even gave private tours of his personal spaces. There were no problems. This wasn't a life-changing event, but for me it was a special treat.

Our group had also been praying for a specific job opportunity for Chuck. We prayed and prayed that he be offered this job. He had a very favorable interview, but he didn't get the job and has continued working in his current position. Recently he said to me,

"I think God was protecting me. The contract for that job is a mess. I think anyone involved with it will be tainted for future positions. It was right that I stay where I am." While the answer wasn't specifically what we'd hoped, it was an answer—and in retrospect, it was success.

In order to track the success of your own Praying Wives Club, we suggest keeping records of prayers requested and answered. My group that met during the writing of this book took on a sanguine shape and despite my admonitions to keep good records, we didn't fully follow the rules. We followed the intent of the law, but not the letter. Yet we still recalled many successes. While we took the summer off due to crazy schedules, we reflected on our experiences with our Praying Wives Club.

Dianne reports,

Once again, God has shown His power to answer our prayers, often in ways that we don't even expect. As I started a new job in radio, I felt so inept that it challenged my confidence. I had left a job in which I was constantly affirmed—and which came naturally to me—to start all over in a new career. I traded success for struggle. Working as a TV anchor was on the opposite end of the spectrum from hosting a radio talk show. The anchor job takes place in a prepared, controlled environment in which I had twenty years' experience. The radio program is a wing-it, entertainment venue—steeped in the very opinions I had been taught not to express in news.

My self-doubt was exaggerated by Mark's ability to do what I couldn't, and do it with seeming ease. He had previously hosted his own radio show and has the personality it takes to engage an audience. I would fret and worry about a topic, trying to figure out what stand to take and what questions to ask to get listeners to call in on the air. Then I would ask him about it, and without any hesitation he would reel off a list of ideas, concepts, and intriguing questions that never occurred to me. I began to whine and talk about quitting.

It was so ironic to us that God had put us in this situation. Mark would have loved to be given the chance to do what I was doing. He could have done my job in his sleep! (The name recognition that I had as a TV anchor is what landed me the job, not my experience or expertise.) Instead, he was struggling in his own way. He had worked to acquire two really good contracts related to his book, but the work was time consuming and intellectually draining. We often asked God, "What do You have in mind for us?"

As Mark and I, and our Praying Wives Club, prayed, the answers to prayer came in subtle yet strong ways. Instead of being critical of my work or discouraged because he didn't get to do it—which was more his nature—Mark began to teach me. He would daily encourage my efforts, pointing out my positive attributes every time I singled out something negative. He highlighted my differences, cheering me on by saying my show didn't need to be the traditional talk radio gig. He helped me find a new niche that played to my strengths, not weaknesses. In years past, I don't think he would have been as supportive. I believe God has worked on his heart during the difficulties that he's faced, leaving him more in tune with how it feels to be down and discouraged.

In the midst of this trial, God moved mightily again. Realizing I needed backup and considering the uniqueness of a husband/wife team, my station offered Mark a job as my cohost. It's a dream opportunity for us, but of course it doesn't come without its own required prayer. To take this position, Mark would have to give up a higher paying contract. We also are hesitant for us both to be employed by the same company. Two incomes from one source can be risky. We feel confident that God has it all worked out. And as life goes on, there will always be new reasons to start, or continue, a Praying Wives Club.

My successes reported in this book have been more of the daily nature. Dianne's successful experiences have been more dramatic, at least more public. In the previous chapter we shared Pam's Praying Wives Club success when she placed a "911" call requesting prayer for a family crisis—another dramatic result. As I prepared to write this chapter, Pam's husband, David, sent the following to me:

> It was encouraging to know that God is at work even when you are so distracted by the surrounding crisis, your human nature is to act before you think. When Pam gave me a copy of the chapter with our story to preview before it went to publication, I saw God at work—our son was found and, while he was disciplined, he was surely not harmed. I did not even know she had called the group until I read the chapter preview. It is a blessing to see how prayers were answered on our behalf, even without knowing others were praying at the time.
>
> As the wives have prayed together, I am proud of my wife for taking this approach, seeking godly women with whom to grow and pray. At first I was a little apprehensive. Just knowing my wife was sharing my/our needs with women I didn't really know, whom I had no control over, and no control over what she told them, was something I wasn't sure I was comfortable with. We men, especially pastor types, must realize we don't have it all together. We all need more prayer. Also, as husbands, we cannot fulfill all of our wives' emotional needs. I will now encourage Pam—and the women in our church—to be part of a group with others who can fill some of those needs in a healthy way—like a Praying Wives Club!

David went from merely agreeing that Pam could participate to being supportive of the entire concept. Their church now has a Praying Wives Club that has put techniques presented in this book into practice. They, too, have had great success!

Becky started her Praying Wives Club and followed the guidelines provided here. While they're nearly finished with their first three-month commitment, they already have at least thirty specific answers to prayers as a result of their Praying Wives Club. Their successes range, too, from the daily to the dramatic. One of their members works for the school system, and she needed income through the summer. They prayed and the financial needs have been met.

One of the ladies needed a new car—and had been needing one for two years. The Praying Wives Club made her car a matter of prayer. In two weeks, she had a new car.

Another had a job interview, and she asked for prayer. The group prayed specifically that she would know "instantly" if this job was right for her. She went to the interview, it went well, and they offered her the job. But she knew instantly that this job was not right for her.

One of the husbands had a job concern. They prayed and his contract was renewed for two years. Another wife wanted to help out in their church and wanted her husband to work with her. He'd been resistant to helping in the church, but the group prayed about it. Within two weeks the husband began serving in the church.

Another answered prayer was about prayer. One of the Praying Wives Club members asked that the wives pray that her husband would be willing to pray with her. They'd been praying separately for twenty-six years, and she was afraid to ask. The group prayed, and the husband and wife are now praying together. I like to think that seeing her pray with her friends influenced his acceptance of praying together.

One lady's father-in-law was in the hospital dying. After the group prayed, he went home and is now doing well.

With these successes, Becky's group, as they approach the end of their first semester, unanimously agreed to re-up. They've committed to another three months. Becky had suggested that they split up and each start a new group, but no one wanted to split up. Becky told me, "I think we are addicted to this. We want to keep going forever." This next semester, they've also agreed to welcome an additional member into the group. She's seen the changes made in the members' marriages and wants to participate as well.

They meet at a nearby Starbucks and even see the meeting place as a powerful part of what they're doing. Becky told me, "Last week we were meeting at Starbucks and some men were watching us. Finally one of them came up to us and asked, 'What are you ladies so intense about over here?' When we told him we were praying for our husbands and our marriages, he was touched and asked if we would pray for him as a husband. We stopped and prayed for him right then and there. By praying in Starbucks, we are a witness."

Through their Praying Wives Club, not only has Becky's group seen prayers answered and experienced changes in their marriages, they've each grown. Several of the women in Becky's group commented that they'd learned to pray or learned to pray Scripture. Tina said she especially appreciated learning to pray Scripture and to pray directly for her husband. She likes looking back through the notebook and seeing all the answered prayers. Nancy agrees: "The Praying Wives Club has taught me to pray. The way I was raised, women didn't pray. It has also given me new and deeper friendships."

Another wife said that the friendships are so deep, and they know each other so well, that even if one member has to miss a meeting, the others know how to pray for that member. Through the months they've prayed together, they've gained new insights into their marriages and their husbands.

Pam is excited to see their successes. She says, "As a pastor's wife I found great joy in sharing the Praying Wives Club concept with the ladies of my church. What a blessing it has been to see these women come together, unite in public prayer, and take a positive, active stand for their marriages. The Praying Wives Club provides them the opportunity to be a light in our church and our community. Way to go, girls!"

A friend of mine who's also a pastor's wife is encouraging some women in her church to start a Praying Wives Club. She thinks that as women come together in confidence to bear one another's burdens, it will greatly ease the load the pastor carries.

All of us have experienced positive changes in our marriages, we have seen prayers answered, and we have deeper friendships as we've carried one another's burdens.

HOW DO I START A PRAYING WIVES CLUB?

Chapter 5

Connection

Part 1: Who Will Be Part of My Praying Wives Club?

In the same way, even though we are many individuals, Christ makes us one body and individuals who are connected to each other.

—Romans 12:5 GWT

You've read about why Dianne, I, and some other wives felt the need to pray for our husbands and our marriages. You've also read about the kinds of support we get and the success we've experienced in praying for our marriages. Maybe you want those same kinds of benefits, and you're thinking about beginning a Praying Wives Club of your own.

In creating the type of connection discussed so far, three elements need to be addressed:

- Who will be a part of your Praying Wives Club?
- Where will you meet?
- When will you meet?

This chapter discusses the "who" question, chapters 6 and 7 discuss the "where" and "when."

Because confidentiality is of utmost importance (confidentiality is covered in chap. 8), we advise that you not simply post a notice in the grocery store, or even in your local Christian bookstore. Prayers that address such personal topics as husbands and marriages are not something to share with just anyone. The women with whom you gather to pray must respect confidentiality and display emotional stability. So it may take some time to gather the women who will make up your Praying Wives Club.

It's logical to begin your Praying Wives Club with women who are already your friends or with whom you have an acquaintance. We are, after all, attracted to people who are similar to us and with whom we feel comfortable. When our original group first connected, we knew each other from our church's women's Bible study. Though we didn't know each other all that well at the time, this common foundation gave us the ability to trust one another right away.

I encourage you to widen your circle—especially for the second "semester" of your Praying Wives Club. The first time around, you may be doing well to get three women who will consistently gather together. As your marriages change, grow, and improve, others will likely want to join you.

When Dianne and I were looking to create a new Praying Wives Club, I sent a copy of the recorded presentation we'd done on the Praying Wives Club to my close circle of friends and invited them to join us in forming a new group. Much to my surprise, none of them responded. Yet at the time we began to write this book, several women in my wider circle of acquaintances wanted to participate.

Many others in a broader circle of contacts also wanted to start Praying Wives Clubs. Tracy, for example, was in the audience the first time Dianne and I spoke on this topic. She has a few girlfriends with whom she walks every day. After hearing our experiences, Tracy wanted the same thing for her marriage. She discussed creating a Praying Wives Club with her walking buddies, and they decided that every Friday they'd stay together a little beyond their walking time to pray for their marriages.

JoDee's father is the pastor at a church that Chuck and I have visited near our new home. She happened to be at my house one day when I started writing this book. "What are you writing?" she asked. I told her the title was *The Praying Wives Club*, and she exclaimed, "Oh, can I come?"

If you're new in your community and don't yet have a group of girlfriends, consider participating in a local Bible study. When I first moved to Albuquerque and didn't know anyone, I made my first friends by attending the Bible study at the church we attended. Your local Christian bookstore or radio station might have information on Bible studies in your area. Once you've selected a study to attend, go faithfully and get to know the people. Listen when they share their prayer requests. If they seem to need prayer for their husbands and/or their marriages, they may be likely candidates for starting a Praying Wives Club.

When you discover someone with whom you feel a connection, suggest going to lunch or out for coffee. As one by one you develop true friendships with these women, they'll become logical candidates to approach about starting a Praying Wives Club.

As you look for others who would benefit from a planned time of purposeful prayer for their marriages, remember that you don't need a big group. For the model of honesty and connection we're suggesting, between three and six members is a workable number; more than six would be unwieldy.

While it's nice to meet with women with whom you have things in common, don't be afraid to seek women who have different circumstances than you. As you read in the opening stories, our original group included members who had many similarities and differences. The three of us were close in age; were professional women with flexible but demanding schedules; had husbands with professional struggles. These similarities helped us bond instantly, and Dianne and I have remained best friends since that time.

The women in our group, however, were not all alike. Neither Dianne nor Mark had been married previously, had no children prior to marriage, and had been married nine years when we began to pray together. I had not been married previously, but Chuck had a short marriage before we met. We had no children and had been married eighteen years. Our third member and her husband both had been married previously. She had no children but he did, and they were newlyweds at the inception of our first Praying Wives Club. So while Dianne's and my biggest marriage stresses revolved around our husbands' careers, her's were stepchildren and ex-wives.

One of our readers, Angie, is thinking of starting a Praying Wives Club with three other women whose age variance is twenty years. Angie has three children, one friend has four, and the other has six. Angie's oldest child is eleven; their oldest are twenty-two and thirty-two, and they've been married fifteen to twenty-five years. All the wives, though, have been Christians about the same length of time, all three of their husbands have their own businesses, and all three of them help with that business from time to time. Otherwise, none of them work outside the home, and two of them home-school their children. They're all very involved with their children and do a lot of volunteer and missions-related work.

Our similarities help us connect, but the differences add richness and depth to our experience. We can all come together as we focus on what unites us: our love for God, our love for our husbands, and our desire to honor our husbands by supporting them in prayer. So as you build your Praying Wives Club, look for people with whom you have things in common, but don't be afraid of differences. You can learn from each other as individuals who are connected.

Be open to a nudge from the Holy Spirit. A woman in the Bible study in which I participated frequently expressed a need for prayer for her marriage. I felt God prompting me to talk to her, but I never did. Now I have no idea where to find her. I've often thought of her—and I pray for her marriage when I do—but I've always regretted that I never reached out to her. So regardless of where you find the women to join with you in prayer, be sure to pray about each potential member, asking God's guidance about whom to approach.

Chapter 6

Connection

Part 2: Where Will We Meet?

As often as possible Jesus withdrew to out-of-the-way places for prayer.

—Luke 5:16 MSG

After you've found your prayer partners, the next step is to decide on a meeting place.

My first Praying Wives Club met at our church . . . for a while. It's a mega-church that's centrally located and has a full espresso bar. The location, however, turned out not to be such a good idea. It made us a little too visible. Prior to her marriage, my friend had worked at the church for a number of years, I'd spoken at several of the church's women's events, and Dianne's face was on TV every night. We were too well-known to pray in a place where we were recognized. People constantly interrupted us, not realizing that we were having more than a social cup of coffee, wanting to join our conversation or just to say hello.

Meeting in any of our homes was not a good option for us, either. We lived on different sides of town, and we often gathered together before or after being out and about for other reasons.

Plus, meeting in one of our homes would have made the Praying Wives Club feel more social. We'd feel compelled to clean the house, bake some goodies, and make coffee. Not that there's anything wrong with that, but for us and our busy schedules, meeting in one of our homes didn't work.

With our first Praying Wives Club and the one taking place during the writing of this book, we found meeting at a Starbucks or a similar, locally owned coffee house was a good choice. They have comfortable seating, and as long as we buy something, they're happy to have us use the space. To avoid interruption Dianne has to sit with her back to the room. Several times we've been actively praying—eyes closed, heads bowed—when someone spots Dianne and interrupts us to say hello to her or to pitch a news story idea.

Visibility may not be a concern for you, but you may be well-known in your neighborhood. If so, you may need to select a spot that doesn't have high traffic. Even if no one knows you prayer can feel awkward in a bustling, public place.

For you, meeting in your home may be the perfect option. Just be sure to turn the ringers off on your phones and let all calls go to voice mail. For Tracy and her walking buddies, mentioned earlier, rotating homes following their walk works well.

You have to find out what works the best for your Praying Wives Club. If you live in a region of the country that has consistently good weather, a local park or other outdoor setting may be a good choice. That's what Sherry does: "When the weather is great, my friend and I take a 'prayer walk' out in the country, through woods, or stop next to some waterfalls. There's nothing like being out in God's country when you talk with Him!" As you think about what type of location will work best for you and your group, why not consider the following:

 ❧ *Restaurants:* Many restaurants have private rooms for special groups. As long as you don't take the space during or near meal times, they might let you use it. Buy a coffee and let them know you don't need any service. If the restaurant manager or owner is a Christian he or she would be even more likely to let you use the room.

❀ *Bookstores:* Try meeting in a bookstore that has a coffee shop. Most people there are reading and not paying any attention to you. There may be fewer people there who could recognize and interrupt you.

❀ *Libraries:* Check with the local library for the rules regarding use of its meeting rooms. Some libraries charge for the rooms and some do not.

❀ *Schools:* Check with a Christian school. You may be able to use a classroom after school lets out or even during the evening when the custodian is there. If you know a school principal who's a Christian, he or she might let you use a classroom after school hours.

❀ *Churches:* Most churches have some sort of office hours. Ask to use an out-of-the-way classroom where you can shut the door and have some privacy during the office hours. Or if you must meet at night, ask to use a classroom on a night when the building will be open for Bible study, scout meetings, or a committee meeting. Choose your classroom away from the activity and shut the door. Some churches have a quiet room furnished specifically as a prayer room and that is accessible to anyone during office hours.

❀ *Businesses:* If you know a real estate office or beauty shop manager/owner, and the business is closed at night, the person might let you use the waiting room.

❀ If you're having trouble locating a place, pray for God to show you one!

Chapter 7

Connection
Part 3: When Will We Meet?

Then when you pray, GOD will answer. You'll call out for help
and I'll say, "Here I am."
—Isaiah 58:9 MSG

The group should decide on the term for which the Praying Wives
Club will convene. We recommend that a Praying Wives Club
meet for a predetermined number of weeks or months, somewhere
between three and six months. If most of the group's members are
moms with school-age children, a semester may be a good way to
determine length. Many women's Bible studies follow the local
school district schedule for their meetings.

If the group is made up of long-time friends, six months may be
a good choice. If the members don't know each other, a shorter
time frame is advisable. People will more easily commit to this
"unknown" club if it's for a short time. Also, among a group who
are unknown to each other, there may not be the connection you
hope for. There may be, for example, doctrinal differences among
the members that create a conflict. In this sort of situation, it's
uncomfortable to tell someone she doesn't fit in. Or someone's life

could take on a sudden change, like a new job, that cuts down on her ability to participate. A predetermined time frame eliminates any of these potentially awkward situations.

Our original group met for about two years, after which time it sort of fizzled out. Our schedules changed, and finding a time to meet got harder and harder. Also, our marriages had settled, minimizing the need to gather together. Since we didn't really know we were creating a "group," we had no rules. It would have been more comfortable to discontinue meeting together if we'd had an official end date.

If all is going well, the group can, of course, take a break and begin again for a new term. At that time, the groups might welcome a new member or two into the group—space permitting.

Depending on who your members are, it may be best to pick a day and time and stick with it every week. On the other hand, you might decide to meet every other week or even once a month. We suggest that you aim for once a week to keep up the connection and continuity. Because the number of members is small, however, you can easily adjust to the needs of the group. Several members of our group have schedules that vary greatly. We agreed that if three of us were available on a given week, we'd go ahead and meet. At the end of each meeting, we figure out when and where we'll meet again. During vacation times or a particularly busy season, we may skip a week or two.

Next, consider how long each meeting will be. Length of meetings will be determined by the available time and number of members. We suggest somewhere between forty-five minutes and two hours. The Praying Wives Clubs I've been part of are made up of women with flexible schedules, so we tend to run closer to two hours and include breakfast or lunch and coffee.

Forming a Praying Wives Club will take a little time and energy, and maybe even some research. When a builder starts a new project, she doesn't just show up somewhere and begin putting up walls.

First she finds a suitable location, and then she ensures that she has faithful workers who will help her and will consistently report to the job. Then those workers can help her build a firm foundation. As you plan to begin your Praying Wives Club, look around your circle of friends and acquaintances, in your church sphere, and allow the Holy Spirit to help you make the connection—where you'll meet, with whom you'll be meeting, and when you'll meet. When these are established, your group can begin building a firm foundation of prayer for your marriages. God will honor your efforts and bless your willingness to pray for your husbands.

What Are Some Concerns for a Praying Wives Club?

Chapter 8

Confidentiality

A gossip goes about telling secrets, but one who is trustworthy in spirit keeps a confidence.

—Proverbs 11:13 NRSV

Question: In a Praying Wives Club meeting, what prayer topics should be kept confidential? Answer: All of them.

When Dianne and I were trying to form our new Praying Wives Club, I sent a recording of our speech on the topic to friends whom I thought might be interested in joining us. One friend told me she and her husband had listened to the tape in their car during a trip. Her husband was hesitant to have her get involved because he was unsure he wanted us to know that much about him. Rightfully, husbands need to be aware of their wives' participation, and out of respect for him, she declined to join us.

When we invited JoDee to join us, she asked her husband for his permission and approval. His answer was immediately supportive. He said, "It will be good for you to have women to pray with— and we could use the prayers."

Pam's husband, David, was concerned at first. He wondered

where Pam's loyalties would lie—would she be more concerned about being honest in sharing with the group, or more concerned with protecting private matters? Pam assured him that private matters would remain private, and that her loyalty was with him. In the safe environment of the Praying Wives Club, we've all sworn to respect each other's confidences. In such surroundings, Pam can share her heart without fear of judgment or gossip. As a pastor's wife, Pam needs this type of outlet—which her husband respects. He gave his blessing.

Lila's husband, Wayne, is very private. She wasn't sure he'd support her interest in joining our Praying Wives Club. She prayed about it before discussing her participation with him. When they did talk about it, she gave him an overview of the concept—including the confidentiality within the group—and asked if he'd like her to pray for him. At that time, Wayne had some serious health concerns, and he said, "Yes, please pray for my health." Inside, Lila was jumping up and down with joy. She knew that there is power when two or more gather together in prayer, and Wayne's positive response was, in itself, an answer to prayer.

Chuck had no concerns about my gathering with girlfriends to pray for our marriage. After more than twenty years of marriage to a speaker/author, he's pretty comfortable with our life's being, literally, an open book. As a licensed professional counselor who specializes in marriage, he's pleased to see me doing something proactive for our marriage and motivating others to do the same.

So Chuck, and JoDee's husband, Donald, were supportive and glad that their wives cared enough about their marriages to make it a prayer priority. Pam's David and Lila's Wayne were a little less enthusiastic but agreed once they understood the concept and confidentiality.

You should, of course, pray about your involvement in a Praying Wives Club. But if you suspect your husband will be more like David and Wayne than like Chuck and Donald, I encourage you to spend time specifically asking God to prepare your husband's heart—as Lila did—before you approach him about your participation.

As Pam did with David, you might also encourage him to read this chapter so he's aware that confidentiality is a priority in a Praying Wives Club. Each member must agree that anything shared within the confines of the group will not be shared with anyone outside the group—including husbands! If you share with your husband, he might think others in the group are sharing with their husbands what you've said about him. This agreement is for perpetuity—forever and ever.

No husband will be comfortable thinking that his wife is going to a hen party full of gossips. When he knows the boundaries of the group—that every member takes confidentiality seriously— he'll probably, like Chuck, be excited to have his wife taking proactive steps in support of their marriage.

Following a Praying Wives Club meeting, JoDee, the newly-wed member of our current group, sheepishly approached me. "I think I shared too much," she said. "I don't think I should have told you all that." I assured her that she needn't worry—that this group was the place for sharing burdens, that not a word of what she told us would go outside the group, that we were concerned for her situation, but did not judge her. Likewise, you can be sure that every story told in this book is shared with permission.

Because of the nature of the group, it's not practical to get permission from each husband for every need that is shared. Topics for prayer may well be discussed that, especially when a member is in a difficult marital place, are private and tender. These delicate matters should be discussed, as the Praying Wives Club is just the place to be able to share your heart.

Such confidentiality excludes, of course, situations in which life is threatened, such as a contemplated suicide, or child abuse, or where such a felony as drug dealing is taking place (not minor infractions like speeding or interpretation of tax laws). To with-hold this information from authorities is likely to put Praying Wives Club members themselves in trouble. Most states require the re-porting of suspected child abuse, and withholding such informa-tion could be considered "obstruction of justice."

If, then, these elements are a part of your personal situation and you want to bring them up for prayer, we suggest that rather than place your sisters in a difficult place, these needs be addressed in a general manner. You might say, "There's a situation in my house-hold about which I am frightened. Please pray for my safety and for God's direction in handling it." Otherwise, unless you need the situation reported, confidences of a "reportable" nature should be kept out of the Praying Wives Club environment. Do, however, seek out help for your situation from a trusted pastor or counselor, or from an appropriate support group. To do so may be difficult, but we strongly encourage you not to leave yourself or your loved ones in a potentially dangerous situation.

In our groups, we haven't struggled with issues related to confi-dentiality. We believe, though, that it's important to set a solid foundation for this vital element of making a Praying Wives Club work. One wife who read the manuscript as we wrote asked about confidentiality. She'd like to start a Praying Wives Club, but one of her friends, whom she knows will want to participate, cannot keep a confidence. Keeping confidences is likely to be a concern for many who wish to start a Praying Wives Club—which is why we've included this chapter.

Ideally, each member of your Praying Wives Club should have her own copy of this book and should have read it. This way, all members start with the same understanding regarding the impor-tance of confidentiality.

We suggest that you adopt the following policy, as we have, for your Praying Wives Club: Each member of the Praying Wives Club has agreed to keep in confidence everything said in the group (see contract at the end of this chapter). If a confidence is betrayed, some corrective action is needed.

The offender needs to apologize to the group as a whole and then more specifically to the person whose trust has been betrayed. Assuming the offender believes she can correct her behavior in the future, she'll promise not to break the confidence again.

She then leaves the group setting and the others vote whether or not she can stay in the group. If even one member feels that she cannot share her heart freely if the offender remains in the group, the offender is not welcomed back into the group.

This may seem harsh. But if all members of the group agree to adhere to this premise and understand the consequences up front, breaking a confidence seldom becomes an issue. This model has been used successfully in many other groups.

When all members agree to keep everything that's shared within the confines of the group, an environment of trust is created. Group members can then share their hearts with confidence and pray for the real concerns that face our marriages.

The dictionary defines contract as "an agreement between two or more parties for the doing or not doing of something specified." As you and your girlfriends gather together, it's important that you have an agreement on certain key principles. As the definition states, this agreement is for the doing and not doing of specific things.

In previous chapters we've outlined some foundational elements that are important to a successful Praying Wives Club. In the following contract, those specifics are enumerated. While each group may determine which items are the most important to it, we recommend that, in the beginning, you simply follow the suggested guidelines. By including these in a contract and requiring each member to read and sign the contract, everyone clearly understands the ground rules.

This contract is presented here in such a way that the leader can easily photocopy it for each member, or each member can copy her own. Once the contract has been reviewed, each woman should sign it. To signify the contract's importance, hold some sort of little signing ceremony. One suggestion would be to have the leader read each point out loud, then have each member sign the contract (or contracts as noted in the next paragraph). Place the copy (or copies) in the center of a table, have each member place a hand on the contract(s), and pray out loud over the contract(s)—either individual prayers or one prayer spoken by the leader.

Your group may choose to make copies of the original signed contract for each member to keep in her Bible or Praying Wives Club journal. Or each member might sign all copies so everyone has her own copy signed by each member. Because confidentiality is so important, we believe that each member should have a fully signed copy of the contract in her possession as a tangible reminder of the commitment she's made.

We encourage each Praying Wives Club member to sign the following contract at the first full meeting.

There are, of course, no Praying Wives Club police who will appear at your meeting should someone violate the agreement. But the act of signing the document validates the importance of the guidelines and indicates acceptance of some basic rules. If you prefer, you may use the text of the following contract as a template, and modify it for the specific needs of your group.

Praying Wives Club Contract

Please review this copy of the contract and arrive at the first meeting of your Praying Wives club ready to sign it with the group.

❀ I commit myself to the Lord Jesus Christ and agree to abide by the precepts of the Bible.

❀ I am committed to my marriage and to supporting the marriages of my sisters in the Praying Wives Club.

❀ I commit to loving my husband by lifting him up and covering him in prayer.

❀ I commit to making the Praying Wives Club a priority in my life for the designated time frame, and having done so will endeavor to be on time for the agreed-upon meeting time.

❀ I commit to being an active and gracious listener as my sisters share their hearts. I ask the Holy Spirit to guide my thoughts and words.

❀ I commit to praying for my friends and their marriages throughout the week—as the Holy Spirit leads me.

❀ I commit to keeping the sacred trust of this Praying Wives Club by not sharing what is spoken here with any other person. I understand that if I violate this trust, I will apologize and may be asked to leave the group.

The Praying Wives Club will meet on a regular basis from _____, 20____ to _____, 20____.

Signed: _____ Signed: _____

Signed: _____ Signed: _____

Signed: _____ Signed: _____

Chapter 9

Considerations

Observe how Christ loved us. His love was not cautious but extravagant. He didn't love in order to get something from us but to give everything of himself to us. Love like that.

—Ephesians 5:2 MSG

Each wife involved in a Praying Wives Club needs to carefully consider her motives. When we first got together, it was suggested that we each read Stormie Omartian's book *The Power of a Praying Wife* (Eugene, Ore.: Harvest House, 1997). We each bought a copy and faithfully read the introduction. The book was helpful in preparing us for the concept that we were not praying to fix our husbands—though I admit the idea had been hovering around the edges of my thoughts.

About praying for your husband, Stormie wrote,

It's laying down all claim to power in and of yourself, and relying on God's power to transform you, your husband, your circumstances and your marriage. This power is not given to wield, like a weapon in order to beat back an unruly beast. It's a gentle

71

tool of restoration appropriated through the prayers of a wife who longs to do more than be right, and to give life more than get even. It's a way to invite God's power into your husband's life for his greatest blessing, which is ultimately yours too.

As we each read those words, it reminded us of why we were gathering: not to fix our husbands, but to fix our attitudes and support our husbands and our marriages.

You've probably heard the expression (often seen on tee shirts) "If Mama ain't happy, ain't nobody happy." Applied to our Praying Wives Club, in inviting God's power to bless your husband, you get blessed—because as Stormie implies, if he's unhappy, so is everyone else.

At the time of Chuck's worst struggles with depression, I was miserable. But rather than asking God to use some "magic wand" to fix Chuck, I asked God to help me support him, encourage him, and understand him. When my attitude changed from critical to helpful, Chuck was more able to share his feelings with me. As a result, our communication improved. So although Chuck was still plagued by depression, my attitude changed and I was no longer miserable.

Dianne found the same thing to be true in regard to Mark. Like Chuck, Mark is a Perfect Melancholy. They are both perfectionists who have a tendency to see the glass as half empty. Mark readily reacts in a strong way when things go wrong. With his chronic headaches and fatigue, he also gets discouraged. Dianne, not knowing how he feels because she's typically healthy and optimistic, often didn't know how to respond when he was at his low points. She often took personally his bouts of silence, thinking he was angry at her, when actually he was struggling just to keep going. By focusing on praying God's greatest blessing on Mark, Dianne learned to be more compassionate and let Mark work through his tough times without her trying to "fix" him. While they still experience times of emotional discomfort in their relationship, these times don't last as long as they used to. Both Dianne and Mark get over those times more quickly now.

Before your girlfriends commit to being a part of the Praying Wives Club, it's important that each of you be on the same page. The purpose of the group is to lift up the husbands in prayer and build up the marriages, allowing God to change your attitudes rather than expecting your husbands to change.

Memorizing Ephesians 5:2 from *The Message* helped remind me of God's principle on marriage versus self: "Observe how Christ loved us. His love was not cautious but extravagant. He didn't love in order to get something from us but to give everything of himself to us. Love like that." I simplify that: "Not to get, but to give."

Once I embraced the concept of what I call "love extravagantly," this is how it played out in my life: Chuck has a large radio-controlled model airplane that's been a part of his life for nearly forty years. He started building it when he was eight and finally finished it twenty years later. We have painstakingly moved it with us to nine different houses, but Chuck has too much of himself invested in it to risk flying it. With a five-foot wing span, the plane cannot be tucked away just anyplace. In our smaller home it hung near the peak of the cathedral ceiling in the family room. Bright red with Red Baron–like decals, it's sure to be noticed. Since the plane is important to Chuck, I've accepted it as a conversation piece—and you can be sure it is!

One day, he took the airplane to a model airplane show. He spent hours cleaning off the dust that had accumulated and clung stubbornly to every surface. The plane was very popular at the show, and he discovered how valuable it really was. Before he put it back on its hook, he wanted to protect it. He covered the body and wings with plastic dry cleaning bags—which had black and yellow advertising on them.

I like my home to look like a showplace. Even having the airplane visible in the house is an act of compromise and love. Having a Red Baron airplane covered with dry cleaning bags that sported advertising went too far. "I'll never be able to entertain again," I wailed to him. After my outburst, which I knew was an overreaction, I went outside to cool down and trimmed my roses. As I took a deep breath, God clearly spoke two words to me: "love extravagantly."

Does it really matter if the airplane has a bag hanging off it? What's more important, that my husband be happy or that I have a lovely home? Hmm—that was tough. *Love extravagantly,* I told myself. I came back in and apologized—ready to accept the dry cleaning bags. Meanwhile, he'd decided that I was right and the bag-covered plane really was ugly. He'd taken the plane down, removed the dry cleaning bags, and was replacing them with clear plastic wrap. It clings tightly to every horizontal curve and doesn't even show!

As Stormie says, when my desire is for my husband's greatest blessing—when my desire is not to get, but to give—I, too, am blessed.

When you and your girlfriends gather for a Praying Wives Club, I urge you all to consider your motives. Can you enter into earnest prayer for your husbands and your marriages, not to get, but to give? If so, you may be surprised at how often both happen!

Chapter 10

Commitment

Commit yourself to the LORD.

—Psalm 22:8 NASB

It's important that your Praying Wives Club is made up of women who are able to make a commitment.

First, these women need to have made a commitment to the Lord. They need to be women whose faith is real and alive. The basic concept behind a Praying Wives Club is to pray, to have God hear those prayers and to answer them. Scripture tells us that in order for us to recognize God's answers, we must know Him. "I know my sheep as the Father knows me. My sheep know me as I know the Father. . . . My sheep respond to my voice, and I know who they are. They follow me, and I give them eternal life" (John 10:14, 27–28 GWT). If you've taken the precautions addressed in chapter 5, it can probably be assumed that the women in your Praying Wives Club have all made a commitment to the Lord. In addition, all members need to be committed to their marriages and to making their marriages work.

In our first Praying Wives Club, we invited a woman who was

separated from her husband. As we shared our hearts with one another, it was apparent to us—based on what she said—that her marriage was salvageable, that her husband was a decent guy, and that it was she who had left. Because the rest of us were each committed Christians and committed to the general concept of marriage—and to ours specifically—we assumed she had those same beliefs at heart.

In our first few weeks together, we offered suggestions to help this woman and her husband get back together. We prayed in earnest for the restoration of their marriage. After a few weeks, she never came back. She didn't want to fix her marriage. Rather, we believe, she was looking for affirmation for leaving.

In my husband's marriage counseling practice, he's found that many of the people who come in for counseling really don't want counsel. They feel a need to be able to tell people, "I tried marriage counseling and it didn't work. So we got a divorce." Counseling is merely something they need to check off their list on the way to the lawyers.

If not all members share a commitment to the marriage, it would be easy to listen to someone's difficulties—excluding physical abuse or other extreme behaviors—and comment, "He's such a louse. I don't know why you stay with him. I think you should just dump him." Maybe he *has* made poor choices. Maybe he *doesn't* currently treat his wife well. It would be easy to jump on that bandwagon and verbally beat him up.

One day Dianne and I were talking with some girlfriends, not in a Praying Wives Club group. She was venting—as girlfriends do with one another—over a current frustration with Mark. One woman asked her, "Is this how you want to live your life? Is this where you want to be in ten years?" The implication was, *He's not likely to change. You may as well think about getting out before you invest any more of your time in this relationship.*

Within a Praying Wives Club environment, a commitment to

marriage is foundational. Girlfriends will offer compassion, support, and prayer. And when we're committed to the Lord, committed to marriage, and committed to prayer, God can do wonderful things. Amazing changes can occur!

What Happens During a Praying Wives Club Meeting?

Chapter 11

Structure

But be sure that everything is done properly and in order.

—1 Corinthians 14:40 NLT

I'm pretty much an outside-the-box thinker. I believe that rules are meant for other people. Yes, I realize many situations need boundaries, and a Praying Wives Club is one for which guidelines are helpful. Depending on your personality, you may adhere to these suggestions closely, follow them in the beginning and then adjust as needed, or throw them out altogether and do your own thing. Although they are only suggestions, we do encourage you to at least seriously consider them. Why reinvent the wheel?

Let's assume you've decided to create a Praying Wives Club. You know who'll be a part of the group, you've decided where you'll be meeting and when, and everyone has agreed to the commitment of confidentiality. Now you're down to the structure: What will you do at the meetings?

One question involves leadership. We encourage a nurturing, cooperative attitude within a Praying Wives Club, but someone usually needs to take some form of leadership position. This position will likely fall to the woman who read this book first and felt a need to gather her girlfriends. She'll be the woman who rounded up the group and made the decision about to where to meet. She'll be the one who made copies of the contract and got them distributed.

Once it forms, however, someone in the group may take to leadership more naturally and will be someone to whom everyone automatically looks for leadership. Whether the leader is the woman who organized the group or a woman with more leadership skills, someone needs to take charge—not to be a boss, but to keep things on track (addressed in the next chapter).

In our original group, my friend who got us together in the first place acted as our unofficial guide and leader. In the current group, I gathered my girlfriends, and the role of leader seems to have fallen on me. Lila, however, has more "secretarial"-type skills. Before we break up, she's the one who says, "When are we meeting next?" She has us pull out our calendars or PDAs and schedule the next meeting. If someone is missing, or had to leave early, Lila assumes the responsibility of relaying the new date and time.

You also need to look at the meeting's agenda. The meeting has two portions: the praise reports and specific prayer requests portion, and the prayer portion. You'll need to determine the length of each according to how many members are present at each meeting. For the sake of keeping the math simple, let's say three members meet for an hour. Each member, then, has a total of twenty minutes in which to first give praise reports and prayer requests, and then to pray specific prayers. This agenda doesn't need to be followed religiously, but it gives you an idea. The leader will need to move the meeting along and be conscientious about the time allotted to each member.

The heart of the meetings should consist of the three main elements: praise and updates, specific requests, and individual prayers. In our group, we begin by having each wife update us on her life. She tells us what's happened since last week (or the last time she was with us) and shares any specific praise reports—especially those pertaining to what we've previously prayed for. At the conclusion of her time, she tells us how we can pray for her this week and shares the Scripture prayer (see chap. 14) she has selected for her specific situation. We each note the Scripture prayer chosen by each member so we can continue to pray that specific prayer for her throughout the week.

Praise reports and prayer requests will take about three-quarters of your meeting time and may need monitoring if keeping on schedule is important. For three members in an hour meeting, each would take about fifteen minutes in the first portion of the meeting for praise reports and prayer requests, then in the second portion of the meeting each would take about five minutes for the specific prayers.

When everyone has shared, we begin the prayer portion of the Praying Wives Club. One member starts and another closes the prayer time. The leader may assign these positions, or members may offer to open or close. If timing is tight and one member has to leave before the prayer time is likely to be finished, that member should pray first. As each person is prompted by the Holy Spirit, she'll pray for the needs of the different members of the group—including her own requests. During each individual's prayer time, she prays the Scripture prayer she selected for her husband.

In our current group, one member has some tax concerns. Lila used to be a CPA, and because of her financial background, the tax concerns of that member weighed more heavily on Lila's heart than on the rest of us. So Lila specifically brought this need to the Lord in her prayers. I may focus on a different member's need. That same week, for example, I was participating in an event Dianne's husband was organizing. The event was a part of her prayer requests, and because of my involvement, I carried the prayer torch for that specific request.

Ideally, each specific request presented will be prayed for at least once during the actual prayer time. The person closing in prayer should cover any needs that haven't been addressed. But because Praying Wives Club members commit to praying for each other throughout the week, each person's needs will be prayed for over and over again.

When you first begin to lay out the details for your group, it may not seem obvious at first what the exact leadership, timing, and agenda should be for your meetings. The important thing is to get started together as a group, agreeing to try a tentative arrangement. Start with the basics described here, and if it doesn't seem to be working after a few weeks, make whatever changes the group seems to think are needed. Be rigid enough in your arrangement to have a plan, but flexible enough to tweak the details to meet the needs of your specific group.

As it develops, each Praying Wives Club will take on a flavor of its own. Some clubs will follow the schedule religiously, while others will use it only as a framework and make their own rules as they go along. It may take a few weeks of trial and error, but before long you'll find yourselves settling into a routine that is comfortable for everyone in the group. Then rejoice in the results as God blesses your time together!

Chapter 12

Staying on Track

But you need to stick it out, staying with God's plan so you'll be there for the promised completion.

—Hebrews 10:36 MSG

One thing is almost certain when women get together—they gab. Our current gathering of girlfriends is highly sanguine. Four of the five are nearly half sanguine. We love to chat. We have our food and/or coffee, do girl stuff like discussing hair color and passing around hand lotion. We've agreed to come early if we want to visit, so we still manage to get in social chitchat.

Someone in your Praying Wives Club, however, may be extra chatty and may want to keep socializing. If all members of your Praying Wives Club have read this book, and understand the concept—that it's not a social hour but specifically for praying for our husbands and marriages—it's much easier to steer the group back to the purpose. The leader may, in fact, have to frequently pull the group back to prayer and away from casual conversation.

I serve as the leader in our group, and when we get off track with socializing, I watch the clock. Depending on the time, I may let the discussion flow for a bit, or I may simply interrupt with a "Yoo-hoo, we need to stay on track here." Because we're all aware of the guidelines, I'm not perceived as being persnickety. JoDee says my reminder is like a pat on the bottom, that we need to get back on track.

It may be a little harder to keep everyone on track when it comes to prayer. There's so much that's worthy of prayer—sick friends and relatives, issues related to terrorism. It's easy to get distracted by other prayer needs. But then you'll run out of time for the requests for which you're really there to pray. Again when everyone has read the guidelines, they know to avoid bringing up tangential concerns.

The leader can use her own discretion in allowing some current and pressing issues to be addressed in prayer. But if one person seems continually to be distracting the group from its prayer purpose, or if the prayer topics seem to be ever widening from the concerns of husbands, marriage, and issues that directly affect the marriage, the leader should redirect the group.

During the time of our current Praying Wives Club, for example, Dianne has started a new job. After fifteen years in television news, her smiling face is now plastered on billboards all over town, touting her afternoon radio talk show on a brand-new station. Dianne has been stressed about this new role. She says, "For years I've been paid not to have an opinion. Now they want me to have an opinion." She's been struggling to make the adjustment, and we've been praying for Dianne's work. But we haven't been praying for her work just to pray for her work. In Dianne's case, her period of stressful adjustment affects her marriage. The overload and her feelings of incompetence spill into life at home, where she has less patience with her husband and children.

In addition, Mark feels frustrated with Dianne's stress. He used to have his own radio show, and he has very strong opinions. He could do Dianne's show with ease and therefore doesn't understand Dianne's stress. We pray for her stress and for success in this new venture, which allows her to work when her kids are in school and be home when they are. We pray for Mark, that he'll have patience and grace for Dianne as she learns her new role. In praying for Dianne's job, we're staying on track, true to the Praying Wives Club purpose.

The hardest area, though, in which to stay on track may be that of offering advice or counsel. As you read in chapter 3, "Support," a valuable benefit of participating in a Praying Wives Club is the support system it provides. Members need to be careful, however, not to turn the meeting into a counseling session. If one member is going through a particularly tough time in her marriage, it would be easy for her concerns to usurp all of the group's attention, week after week.

Likewise, one member may have a strong personality and is occupying all the time. Or perhaps another member is the more choleric type, and she may—with good intentions—become the "know it all," having answers for everyone's problems. The leader will need to interrupt and move the meeting on to prevent chatty members from taking over while quieter members never have the opportunity to share. It's important, then, that the schedule from day one allots only a certain number of minutes to each person.

Group members should, of course, offer support and advice from their personal wells of experience. What has one member done that has worked when in a situation similar to that of another member? Or one member may know someone who can offer a solution to another member's problem.

One week, Pam shared about an incident that had become a problem between her and David. He had told her about a lunch meeting with another couple in their church. The meeting was on her day off from work. So she interrupted her yard work and got dressed up to go out to lunch with her husband and this other couple.

When she showed up at her husband's office, he looked at her with an expression that said, "What are you doing here?" It turns out that the other couple had a schedule conflict and the lunch was off. Pam suggested that since she was there and all dressed up, she and David should go to lunch. But David had other tasks to do and didn't want to. Pam felt rebuffed. She went home, changed back into her garden clothes, and weeded the garden with, I'm sure, a great deal of vigor.

Needless to say, this was a minor matter and Pam got over it. But it could have been avoided with clear scheduling. Chuck and I have had similar conflicts. So from my well of experience, I offered her a suggestion: Chuck and I keep a calendar on the wall in the bathroom, next to the toilet—where we have to look at it. We note on it any out-of-town travel and any appointments that involve both of us. That way we're clear on what we're doing. If Pam and David had this system, and he'd written the lunch on the calendar and not crossed it off, he'd clearly need to apologize. If he'd made the change when the lunch was cancelled, Pam would have known—preventing the problem.

From our common wells of experience, we can offer each other insights and solutions. We can pray for each other and the unique needs of each marriage, but we stay on track and avoid getting enmeshed with specific sagas.

Sometimes counseling is needed, but the Praying Wives Club is not the place for that. When deeper conflicts arise in a marriage, encourage group members to seek counsel from their pastor or a professional with the expertise to deal with that situation.

All of us these days are on tight schedules and time is of the essence. By respecting each member's time and not wasting it on matters other than what you came for, your meetings will be more productive and members are more likely to stay committed. Staying on track will keep your Praying Wives Club, as promised, an enjoyable and rewarding experience for everyone!

Chapter 13

Specific Requests

Share each other's troubles and problems, and in this way obey
the law of Christ.

—Galatians 6:2 NLT

A further benefit of a Praying Wives Club is that of following
Christ's teachings by sharing one another's burdens. As discussed
in chapter 11, "Structure," the Praying Wives Club format allows
for the sharing of specific troubles and problems in the form of
prayer requests. Those requests are prayed for during the group
time, and we encourage you to continue praying for one another
through the week—and for as long as the prayer is needed.

To keep the specific prayers active, we suggest keeping a Praying Wives Club journal. In the prayer journal, record each member's
specific requests and selected Scripture prayers. How I wish we'd
done this in our first Praying Wives Club. We had so many answers to prayers, but now, most of them are forgotten.

Please learn from our mistakes. Each member should bring with
her to the meeting a notebook or journal that she keeps specifically
for the Praying Wives Club. Each member starts each meeting with

a fresh page and records each wife's specific requests, leaving room in the margin to note the date and other information about the answer God provides to that prayer. You are, after all, as Mark 11:24 encourages, praying with expectation: "That's why I tell you to have faith that you have already received whatever you pray for, and it will be yours" (GWT).

If you journal and typically write out your prayers, you might follow Lila's example. Throughout the week, during her regular prayer time, Lila prays for each of the specific requests within the Praying Wives Club. In her Praying Wives Club journal, she writes out her prayers as she prays—including writing out each selected Scripture prayer. This helps her stay focused and cover each specific request in prayer. At the next meeting, she turns the page to a clean sheet, dates the page, and begins that week's recording.

What a wonderful way to share each other's troubles and problems! And what a blessing to see God work in each member's life and to see Him answer prayers week by week. Being able to reflect on what God has done in our lives strengthens our faith in future times of trial and testing. As a written account of God's workings, your journal will not only be for record keeping and organizational purposes, it will also be a testimony to the faithfulness, grace, and mercy of God. With that testimony, you can encourage others whom God brings into your path.

I wish I were a journaler like Lila, because I love the record it creates. But that doesn't fit my lifestyle. That doesn't mean, however, that I don't honor the other members' prayer requests. Like Lila, I make note of each person's specific requests and the Scripture prayers each member selected for that week. I make a document for each week that contains the names of all members of the group with each husband's name included. Under each couple's names, I type in the specific prayer request as well as the selected Scripture prayer with the husband's name in the blank space shown in the suggested Scripture prayers. In some cases, because I'm praying for someone other than myself, the prayer as printed in appendix A needs slight tweaking. Once the prayers are adjusted and included in the document, I print out several copies. I keep one next to my bed, one in the car, and one in my purse. As time permits, I pray the specific Scripture prayers for the club members throughout the week.

Another method of keeping track of requests will work well if each member of your Praying Wives Club has her own copy of this book. Simply write each person's name and the date next to the Scripture prayer in appendix A, fold down the corner of that page, and refer to that prayer. As each wife prays, she will insert the name of the members' husbands, making appropriate adjustments in the text because you all will be praying for other husbands, not your own. Another option is to use the Post-it Note colored flags, selecting one color for each group member. As the Scripture prayers are selected each week, simply move the colored flags to the prayer that each wife chose for that week.

Becky made up a notebook for each of the five ladies—including herself—participating in the Praying Wives Club. Each notebook has a copy of the confidentiality contract—with all the signatures—as the first page. The next section of their notebooks contains the Scripture prayers, and they use the Post-it Note flag method mentioned in the previous paragraph. The last section is the prayer diary where they record requests and answers.

Others have suggested making prayer cards for each member of your Praying Wives Club. Each Scripture prayer is written out on a card along with the verse on which it's based, and the cards are kept in a card-catalog type box. The cards are arranged by topic, as they are in appendix A. As each wife selects her Scripture prayer for that week, that card is removed from the box and kept out as a prayer reminder for the week. Notes about the request and its answer can be made on the back of the card. At the conclusion of each meeting, each member takes home with her a prayer reminder card to use throughout the week, and the notations will keep a record of God's work in the group.

It doesn't matter how you remember the specific requests of your Praying Wives Club members. Your ongoing prayers will be a blessing to them and an encouragement to you as you see God respond with His perfect answers!

Chapter 14

Scripture Prayers

And when two or three of you are together because of me, you
can be sure that I'll be there.

—Matthew 18:20 MSG

As you and your girlfriends gather together to pray for your husbands and your marriages, your prayers will reflect the specific
needs you are each facing that week. As you take time to pray for
one another, we recommend incorporating Scripture prayers into
your conversation with God. When you pray Scripture, you know
your prayers are in accordance with God's will.

In appendix A at the back of this book are Scripture prayers that
address a variety of areas in which your marriage and your husband are likely to need prayer. To help you feel comfortable with
these prayers and make it easy for you to incorporate them into
your prayer time, we've chosen to use three particular versions of
the Bible on which to base these prayers: *The Message, The New Living Translation,* and *The Amplified Bible.* In the appendix, the prayer is
listed first—which closely follows the heart message of the verses
used—followed by the actual Scripture on which the prayer is

based. In this way you can learn how to pray Scripture on your own. Most prayers are based on one specific passage of Scripture; some, however, are founded on two or more different passages. In such cases, all verses are included with the prayer. Occasionally, two versions of the Bible are drawn from in writing these prayers. Again, each version is included.

As you pray for one another, speak to God as you would a friend, sharing the needs and concerns of each member of the group. As you pray for your own husband, we suggest that within your prayer, you incorporate one—or more—of the Scripture prayers chosen by each Praying Wives Club member. Prior to gathering with your girlfriends, you could select from this list of Scripture prayers the one that best suits your current situation and then share it with the group as you update them on your praises and needs. As your meeting comes to the prayer time, insert your husband's name in the space provided and pray that prayer specifically for him.

These Scripture prayers aren't necessarily intended to be a prayer all by themselves. They don't, therefore, each start with "Dear God" (or something like that) and end with "Amen." They can, though, easily be used as a prayer all by themselves. Each week, you may wish to write the prayer you selected for your husband on a card or sticky-note that you can put on your bathroom mirror or on your car dashboard, reminding you to pray that prayer for your husband throughout the day. In addition, as a group you could agree to pray one another's specific Scripture prayers throughout the week.

Each week, for example, each member in my Praying Wives Club selects a Scripture prayer that each believes fits her current needs. We share the selected Scripture prayers with each other, and then in our prayer time each wife prays what she selected for her husband. Chuck's employment is now secure, but the week an exciting new opportunity presented itself I asked the group members to pray about this possible position. I selected for Chuck the Scripture prayer based on Proverbs 22:29: "Chuck is diligent and skillful in his work. May he always be in demand and admired." That same week, Dianne's husband had accepted a new contract that he felt was a bit out of his scope of expertise. As a result he was feeling apprehensive—but excited for the challenge. She chose the Scripture prayer based on Deuteronomy 31:8 and Joshua 1:9: "As Mark faces this day, remind him that You go before him. You will be with him. You will never leave him or let him down. Whenever he is faced with fearful circumstances, may he be strong and courageous, not afraid or discouraged."

Each week, each member of our group picks an appropriate Scripture prayer for her husband. As we go around the table—our prayer circle—we pray from our hearts for one another, and then we each pray the specific Scripture prayer we've selected for our own husbands. Each husband is prayed for several times. Then we note the Scripture prayers that each wife has selected so we can pray those prayers for one another throughout the week. Don't be surprised to find that praying for the other members of your group will help your own marriage.

As Dianne and I began to look for the verses to use here and write out the prayers that corresponded with each passage of Scripture, I tried them out—inserting Chuck's name silently in my head as I wrote. While I wasn't really "praying"—and the prayers I was writing didn't necessarily relate to my current marital needs—I found my attitude softening. Satan is fond of testing us in the exact areas we claim to have conquered. As I sat down to write a book that will strengthen marriages everywhere, I was unhappy with Chuck. But as I simply read these prayers, inserting his name, I realized my attitude had changed. Now I'm not even sure what I was angry about— and that was just a few weeks before writing the prayers.

The women who read the drafts of these prayers as they helped Dianne and me write them, told me that the exercise was helpful to them. Wendy wrote, "Prayer 9 in the 'Work' section was probably the most impacting prayer I've read so far. I was brought to tears on this one. Mike and I have completely opposite careers (he is in finances, and I deal with words and graphic design). I tend to 'glaze' over when he starts discussing spreadsheets, budget allocations, and monthly cost projections. Often, I hear the mumbling of the Charlie Brown teacher instead of Mike's words. His lips are moving, but my selfishness is not letting me hear a word he is saying. This prayer reminded me that I need to be a good listener and share in his enthusiasm, even if it is not my way of doing things. I need to show him by my attentiveness that it is important to me because it is important to him."

Because I know of the power of prayer, I trust you'll have a similar experience. Please review the suggested Scripture prayers found in the appendix—and even pray the appropriate ones as you review. Then select the one that is most fitting to your current needs for this week's Praying Wives Club meeting.

Pray your heart.
Pray Scripture.
Pray often.

Chapter 15

Summation

The Praying Wives Club Works

How would you measure the success of a Praying Wives Club? Would you think it successful if members willingly offer each other emotional and tangible support? Would you think it was a success if marriages weathered storms and were strengthened? Would you think it was a success if prayers were answered? For all of us involved in a Praying Wives Club, we could shout a resounding "yes!" We have experienced success!

Remember Tracy with the walking buddies version of the Praying Wives Club? She sent me this report as a follow-up. It testifies to the support that members give each other:

Starting a PWC helped us keep the men in our lives "covered in prayer." Even in the weeks that we missed our prayer time together, we found each other lifting these husbands up in our personal prayer times. This is an action that we can honestly say was unlikely to have happened previously simply because of the busyness of life. Now that we are meeting together regularly to pray for our marriages and for our husbands, these men and their burdens are on our minds and in our hearts—even when we are apart. We have begun to "carry them around with us" and in doing so have put feet to the verse that reads "Bear one another's burdens, and thus fulfill the law of Christ" (Gal. 6:2 NASB).

To facilitate this kind of support, we suggest that each member of your Praying Wives Club keep each other's phone numbers programmed into your cell and home phones so you can easily reach out to one another. Be responsible, of course, in the use of this privilege. Don't be like the little boy who cried "wolf." Call on your club members when you are faced with a real marital "wolf," but otherwise, confine your sharing to times when you and your girlfriends gather for your Praying Wives Club meeting.

If you're ready to bear one another's burdens, gather your girlfriends and pray for your marriages. Using the guidelines and Scripture prayers in this book can help you on the road to success. Looking back on our experience, Pam agrees: "The manner in which the prayers are written with Scripture topics gave me a place to land with my sometimes scattered thoughts. Being able to place one of our husbands' names in the prayer selections brought life and even new meaning to otherwise less-specific Scriptures."

A Praying Wives Club not only deepens your friendships, it strengthens your marriage. Lila bears witness to how praying has had an impact on her marriage:

> I looked forward to the Praying Wives Club prayer times because my husband was having one health problem after another. I know we're married for good in sickness and in health, but continual sickness puts a constant strain on a marriage. Not only did I feel strengthened going to God in prayer for my husband, but praying for my husband's requests with other wives also gave me more compassion for my husband's health. It gave me more patience with my husband when he was tired, anxious, and frustrated due to his ongoing health problems. Also, when other wives asked for prayers for their husbands' health issue, I had

more understanding and compassion for both the other wives and their husbands. Not that I would wish ill health for any of the other husbands, but when other wives asked for prayers for their husbands' health, it helped me feel less alone and more like a sister in Christ with the other wives.

Husbands, too, realize the value of a Praying Wives Club. JoDee's husband, Donald, as his "thank you" to all of us, wrote this to JoDee: "My influence in society has increased. A big part of that can be attributed to you supporting me as the biblical wife that is modeled in Proverbs 31."

All of us have experienced positive changes in our marriages, have seen prayers answered, and have deeper friendships as we have carried one another's burdens. Are you ready for the wonderful things God can do in your marriage? Would you like to see amazing changes? With a genuine commitment to God, to your marriage, and to your husband, gather your girlfriends and pray for your marriage! It's not a social club, it's a Praying Wives Club!

Appendix A

Scripture Prayers

Meanwhile, the moment we get tired in the waiting, God's Spirit is right alongside helping us along. If we don't know how or what to pray, it doesn't matter. He does our praying in and for us, making prayer out of our wordless sighs, our aching groans.

—Romans 8:26 MSG

Please review the following Scripture prayers. Then for each week's Praying Wives Club meeting, select one that is most fitting to your current needs. These Scripture prayers can also be a valuable resource in times of crisis when you can't seem to find the right words.

A. Commitment

(A1)   The world is full of temptations and our society takes wedding vows so lightly. Please help _____ to be fully committed to the vows we took. May we both loosen our family ties and cling only to each other and truly cherish each other. Help us to think, work, and walk in complete unison as we follow Your commands.

And this is why a man leaves father and mother and cherishes his wife. No longer two, they become "one flesh."

—Ephesians 5:31 MSG

❀ ❀ ❀

(A2)   The world says I must be my own woman—strong, independent, and in control. But Your plan is different. _____ and I are one and should be a solid team. Help _____ to give over control of his body, trusting that I will not abuse that privilege. And show me how to receive that privilege without abusing it. Give us both a better understanding of how to serve each other, with proper intentions.

Marriage is not a place to "stand up for your rights." Marriage is a decision to serve the other, whether in bed or out.

—1 Corinthians 7:4 MSG

❀ ❀ ❀

(A3)   Help _____ to understand how to build our marriage based on walking hand in hand. Likewise, help me stop, take his hand, and try to understand. Open up his conversation to me so that we can share our dreams with each other and so that together we move forward. Give him courage to talk out his thoughts with me, and give me grace to hold back my speech while I listen.

Can two people walk together without agreeing on the direction?

—Amos 3:3 NLT

❀ ❀ ❀

(A4)   I feel like everything is trying to tear us apart, yet You brought us together and made us one. Give _____ the strength, courage, and wisdom to close his ears to worldly counsel and keep our commitment. Help me to stand strong alongside him.

Since they are no longer two but one, let no one separate them, for God has joined them together.

—Matthew 19:6 NLT

B. Contentment/Success

(B1)   Some days _____ feels like life is not worth living. He is searching for something to make him feel fulfilled. Help him embrace his faith and trust in You, God. May it help him understand and form a firm foundation upon which he can build his life.

The fundamental fact of existence is that this trust in God, this faith, is the firm foundation under everything that makes life worth living. It's our handle on what we can't see.

—Hebrews 11:1 MSG

❀ ❀ ❀

(B2)   Lord, _____ is my best friend, my love, and my soul mate. What a blessing to be paired with a mate who is also my friend. Please keep him healthy and strong—especially his soul. Bless him in everything he does. Help him to be prosperous in his everyday affairs. May he see and know that his prosperity comes from You.

We're the best of friends, and I pray for good fortune in everything you do, and for your good health—that your everyday affairs prosper, as well as your soul!

—3 John 1:2 MSG

❀ ❀ ❀

(B3)   It is so easy in today's society to get caught up in material-ism, in acquiring all the "stuff" we are told we *must* have. Please keep _____ from these lies. Help him to real-ize that he doesn't need more "stuff." Help him keep his life steeped in Your reality. Help him feel fulfilled so he does not think he is missing out on what others may have. Make that _____'s number one priority, because we know that if it is, You will add everything else we need.

Steep your life in God-reality, God-initiative, God-provisions. Don't worry about missing out. You'll find all your everyday human concerns will be met.

—Matthew 6:33 MSG

❀ ❀ ❀

(B4)   Material possessions are something the world promises as a partner to success. Help _____ remember that we are not defined by what we have, even when we have a lot. Wanting more is greed. Help _____ be content with the blessings You have given us.

Speaking to the people, he went on, "Take care! Protect yourself against the least bit of greed. Life is not defined by what you have, even when you have a lot."

—Luke 12:15 MSG

❀ ❀ ❀

(B5)   May _____ learn to think like Jesus, who, like
          _____, faced many hard times. We always want to
          get our own way, free from difficulties. Yet those difficul-
          ties make us more like Christ, desiring to leave sinful hab-
          its, and anxious to do the will of God. This is my prayer for
          _____.

*So then, since Christ suffered physical pain, you must arm yourselves with the
same attitude he had, and be ready to suffer, too. For if you are willing to
suffer for Christ, you have decided to stop sinning. And you won't spend the
rest of your life chasing after evil desires, but you will be anxious to do the will
of God.*

                                                —1 Peter 4:1–2 NLT

                            ✿ ✿ ✿

(B6)   _____ is worried about some circumstances in his life
          that I can do nothing about. God, I am concerned for him.
          Please take over for me as I lift _____ to You
          and leave him in Your care, because I know You love him
          and know what is best for him. I turn him and all the cir-
          cumstances over to You. May my petitions and praise cre-
          ate in him a sense of wholeness, knowing that everything
          will come together for good as he makes You—not worry—
          the center of his life.

*Don't fret or worry. Instead of worrying, pray. Let petitions and praises shape
your worries into prayers, letting God know your concerns. Before you know
it, a sense of God's wholeness, everything coming together for good, will come
and settle you down. It's wonderful what happens when Christ displaces worry
at the center of your life.*

                                                —Philippians 4:6–7 MSG

❀ ❀ ❀

(B7)   May _____experience the great wealth of contentment, the rich simplicity of being himself. Our world puts such pressure on a man, especially, to climb the career ladder, receive the promotion, and make it to the top. May he not fall into temptation and become trapped by foolish and harmful desires. Touch _____'s heart often, and remind him that it is not worldly recognition, status, and finance that make him successful.

Yet true religion with contentment is great wealth. After all, we didn't bring anything with us when we came into the world, and we certainly cannot carry anything with us when we die. So if we have enough food and clothing, let us be content. But people who long to be rich fall into temptation and are trapped by many foolish and harmful desires that plunge them into ruin and destruction. For the love of money is at the root of all kinds of evil. And some people, craving money, have wandered from the faith and pierced themselves with many sorrows.

—1 Timothy 6:6–10 NLT

❀ ❀ ❀

(B8)   Everywhere we turn, the world tells us that we must have "everything" to be happy. Help _____ not to buy into that lie, that he may be content with whatever he has— whether it is plenty or little.

I know how to live on almost nothing or with everything. I have learned the secret of living in every situation, whether it is with a full stomach or empty, with plenty or little.

—Philippians 4:12 NLT

✿ ✿ ✿

(B9) _____ is a man of character. Help him be free from greed and a craving for earthly possessions. May he be satisfied with what he has. Help _____ embrace Your truth, that You will not leave him without support or leave him helpless.

Let your character or moral disposition be free from love of money [including greed, avarice, lust, and craving for earthly possessions] and be satisfied with your present [circumstances and with what you have]; for He [God] Himself has said, I will not in any way fail you nor give you up nor leave you without support. [I will] not, [I will] not, [I will] not in any degree leave you helpless nor forsake nor let [you] down (relax My hold on you)! [Assuredly not!]

—Hebrews 13:5 AMP

✿ ✿ ✿

(B10) May _____ embrace life today, experiencing the abundant life that Christ came to provide for him. May he have a taste of the eternal life You have for him—more and better than he could ever dream of. At the same time, keep him alert to the devices of the enemy who has come to steal, to kill, and to destroy.

A thief is only there to steal and kill and destroy. I came so they can have real and eternal life, more and better life than they ever dreamed of.

—John 10:10 MSG

✿ ✿ ✿

(B11)   Remind _____ that You have good plans to take care of
        him and not abandon him. May _____ live today in light
        of Your plans that include giving him hope and strength
        for the journey, as well as a wonderful confidence for the
        future.

*For I know the thoughts and plans that I have for you, says the Lord, thoughts
and plans for welfare and peace and not for evil, to give you hope in your
final outcome.*

                                           —Jeremiah 29:11 AMP

(B12)   Please bless _____ with Your security and protection.
        May he feel the gift of Your special smile upon him
        throughout the day, and may Your grace and mercy fill his
        heart and spirit. Please show him Your favor and make him
        prosper.

*GOD bless you and keep you, GOD smile on you and gift you, GOD look you
full in the face and make you prosper.*

                                           —Numbers 6:24–26 MSG

(B13)   We are blessed to have what we truly need, yet _____
        is filled with a sense of discontentment. Please help him
        learn to be happy whether he has much or little.

*Not that I was ever in need, for I have learned how to get along happily
whether I have much or little.*

                                           —Philippians 4:11 NLT

C. Emotions

(C1)   *Anger:* Give _____ a desire to refrain from friendships
with short-tempered people, because a bad temper is con-
tagious and becoming like them could endanger his soul.
When he is in a volatile situation, may he control his anger
and avoid making mistakes. May he defuse the anger of
others with a gentle response.

*Keep away from angry, short-tempered people, or you will learn to be like
them and endanger your soul.*
—Proverbs 22:24–25 NLT

*Those who control their anger have great understanding; those with a hasty
temper will make mistakes.*
—Proverbs 14:29 NLT

A gentle response defuses anger, but a sharp tongue kindles a temper-fire.
—Proverbs 15:1 MSG

❀ ❀ ❀

(C2)   *Worry:* You know _____ better than he does, better than
I do. You are greater than his worries. Right now he is facing debilitating self-criticism. Though there may be some
areas in which he can improve, help him focus on real love
and live in Your reality.

*My dear children, let's not just talk about love; let's practice real love. This is
the only way we'll know we're living truly, living in God's reality. It's also the
way to shut down debilitating self-criticism, even when there is something to
it. For God is greater than our worried hearts and knows more about us than
we do ourselves.*
—1 John 3:18–20 MSG

❀ ❀ ❀

(C3) *Fear:* As _____ faces this day, remind him that You go
before him. You will be with him. You will never leave him
or let him down. Whenever he is faced with fearful circumstances, may he be strong and courageous, not afraid
or discouraged.

*GOD is striding ahead of you. He's right there with you. He won't let you
down; he won't leave you. Don't be intimidated. Don't worry.*
                                        —Deuteronomy 31:8 MSG

*I command you—be strong and courageous! Do not be afraid or discour-
aged. For the LORD your God is with you wherever you go.*
                                        —Joshua 1:9 NLT

❀ ❀ ❀

(C4) *Depression:* _____ is in his prime, yet he stumbles and
falls. He is tired and weak. He is in despair, his spirit has
drained away, and his heart is heavy. He feels as though he
has hit bottom. He feels that Your love for him has run out,
that Your mercy has dried up. God, he is nearly at the end
of his rope. Please do not turn away from him, don't ignore
him. That would be certain death. He needs to recover his
life. Help him get away with You so he can experience real
rest. Help him keep company with You that he might learn
to live freely and lightly. Bring him to You quickly, Lord, as
his depression deepens. I trust You to speak to him of Your
unfailing love. I have come to You in prayer on his behalf.
Show us each where to walk.

I'll never forget the trouble, the utter lostness, the taste of ashes, the poison I've swallowed. I remember it all—oh, how well I remember—the feeling of hitting the bottom. But there's one other thing I remember, and remembering, I keep a grip on hope: GOD's loyal love couldn't have run out, his merciful love couldn't have dried up.

—Lamentations 3:19–22 MSG

For even young people tire and drop out, young folk in their prime stumble and fall.

—Isaiah 40:30 MSG

He gives power to those who are tired and worn out; he offers strength to the weak.

—Isaiah 40:29 NLT

Are you tired? Worn out? Burned out on religion? Come to me. Get away with me and you'll recover your life. I'll show you how to take a real rest. Walk with me and work with me—watch how I do it. Learn the unforced rhythms of grace. I won't lay anything heavy or ill-fitting on you. Keep company with me and you'll learn to live freely and lightly.

—Matthew 11:28–30 MSG

I sat there in despair, my spirit draining away, my heart heavy, like lead. I remembered the old days, went over all you've done, pondered the ways you've worked. . . . Hurry with your answer, GOD! I'm nearly at the end of my rope. Don't turn away; don't ignore me! That would be certain death. If you wake me each morning with the sound of your loving voice, I'll go to sleep each night trusting in you. Point out the road I must travel; I'm all ears, all eyes before you.

—Psalm 143:4–5, 7–8 MSG

I am losing all hope; I am paralyzed with fear. I remember the days of old. I ponder all your great works. I think about what you have done. . . . Come

quickly, LORD, and answer me, for my depression deepens. Don't turn away
from me, or I will die. Let me hear of your unfailing love to me in the morning, for
I am trusting you. Show me where to walk, for I have come to you in prayer.
—Psalm 143:4–5, 7–8 NLT

☘ ☘ ☘

(C5)   *Self-worth:* Lord, remind _____ of just how valuable he is to You. Let him know he was created as Your masterpiece, according to Your design, and that no one knows him like You do. Assure _____ that You are concerned with and aware of even the smallest details in his life. Nothing is hidden from You as he is forever in Your thoughts and is precious in Your sight. Open my eyes so that I always see the best in _____, that I may see in him what You see. Let my words and actions always be affirming, loving, and uplifting, never condemning or demeaning. With this foundation, may he do the good things You have prepared him for and have planned for his life.

For we are God's masterpiece. He has created us anew in Christ Jesus, so that
we can do the good things he planned for us long ago.
—Ephesians 2:10 NLT

You know me inside and out, you know every bone in my body; You know
exactly how I was made, bit by bit, how I was sculpted from nothing into
something. Like an open book, you watched me grow from conception to birth;
all the stages of my life were spread out before you, the days of my life all
prepared before I'd even lived one day. Your thoughts—how rare, how beau-
tiful! God, I'll never comprehend them! I couldn't even begin to count them—
any more than I could count the sand of the sea. Oh, let me rise in the morning
and live always with you!
—Psalm 139:15–18 MSG

Not even a sparrow, worth only half a penny, can fall to the ground without your Father knowing it. And the very hairs on your head are all numbered. So don't be afraid; you are more valuable to him than a whole flock of sparrows.

—Matthew 10:29–31 NLT

❀ ❀ ❀

(C6) *Pride:* The world encourages us to have assurance in our own resources and the stability of earthly things, which is the pride of life. Instead of falling prey to these habits of the arrogant, help _____ do Your will and carry out Your purpose for his life; that he will honor Your name, that You will dawn on him—bursting with energy!

For all that is in the world—the lust of the flesh [craving for sensual gratification] and the lust of the eyes [greedy longings of the mind] and the pride of life [assurance in one's own resources or in the stability of earthly things]— these do not come from the Father but are from the world [itself]. And the world passes away and disappears, and with it the forbidden cravings (the passionate desires, the lust) of it; but he who does the will of God and carries out His purposes in his life abides (remains) forever.

—1 John 2:16–17 AMP

Count on it: The day is coming, raging like a forest fire. All the arrogant people who do evil things will be burned up like stove wood, burned to a crisp, nothing left but scorched earth and ash—a black day. But for you, sunrise! The sun of righteousness will dawn on those who honor my name, healing radiating from its wings. You will be bursting with energy, like colts frisky and frolicking.

—Malachi 4:1–2 MSG

❀ ❀ ❀

(C7)   *Sound Mind:* It is easy for _____ to see the worst and the
        ugly, to curse when things do not go his way. Help him
        learn from Your example. Help him fill his mind with the
        best and the beautiful, to look for things to praise. May he
        learn to meditate on the things that are true, noble, repu-
        table, authentic, compelling, and gracious. As he does this,
        please make everything work together and fit into Your
        most excellent harmony.

*Summing it all up, friends, I'd say you'll do best by filling your minds and
meditating on things true, noble, reputable, authentic, compelling, gracious—
the best, not the worst; the beautiful, not the ugly; things to praise, not things
to curse. Put into practice what you learned from me, what you heard and
saw and realized. Do that, and God, who makes everything work together,
will work you into his most excellent harmonies.*

—Philippians 4:8–9 MSG

D. Finances

(D1)   Help _____ to put his whole heart into storing up his
        treasures in heaven rather than stockpiling the things of
        the world that are threatened by moths, rust, and burglars.
        May heaven be the place he wants to end up being.

*Stockpile treasure in heaven, where it's safe from moth and rust and burglars.
It's obvious, isn't it? The place where your treasure is, is the place you will
most want to be, and end up being.*

—Matthew 6:20–21 MSG

✿ ✿ ✿

(D2)   Thank You, Father, for all that You have allowed us to gain. Thank You for the strength You give _____. Help him recognize that whatever earthly riches we have come from You. Do not ever let him become prideful and think that he is a "self-made man," but rather may he always be aware that whatever we have is a gift from You.

If you start thinking to yourselves, "I did all this. And all by myself. I'm rich. It's all mine!"—well, think again. Remember that GOD, your God, gave you the strength to produce all this wealth so as to confirm the covenant that he promised to your ancestors—as it is today.
                                              —Deuteronomy 8:17–18 MSG

⚘ ⚘ ⚘

(D3)   Help _____ function within Your economy. The world's economics say to get what you can, but You tell us that to get, we must give. Help _____ give in large ways. Bless us with full measure so that we have to press it down, shake it together—to make room for more, and even so it is running over.

If you give, you will receive. Your gift will return to you in full measure, pressed down, shaken together to make room for more, and running over. Whatever measure you use in giving—large or small—it will be used to measure what is given back to you.
                                              —Luke 6:38 NLT

⚘ ⚘ ⚘

(D4)   Teach _____ how to be faithful in the small things as well as the big things in his life. Help him to be honest in every dealing he has so that he will be known as a man of integrity

and will be one others can look up to and trust. Give him the
strength to say no to even the tiniest compromise in all he
does. May he choose to serve You and not money.

*Unless you are faithful in small matters, you won't be faithful in large ones. If
you cheat even a little, you won't be honest with greater responsibilities. And if
you are untrustworthy about worldly wealth, who will trust you with the
true riches of heaven? And if you are not faithful with other people's money,
why should you be trusted with money of your own? No one can serve two
masters. For you will hate one and love the other, or be devoted to one and
despise the other. You cannot serve both God and money.*

—Luke 16:10–13 NLT

❧ ❧ ❧

(D5)   May _____ feel the richness of being himself before God.
May he enjoy the wealth that comes with right living. You
brought him into this world with nothing, and he will leave
this world with nothing. We are blessed to have the neces-
sities of life. Please keep _____ from giving in to the lure
of the almighty dollar. Help him to do his job well and to
provide adequately for us, but help him to work with balance and to not become obsessed with gaining more and
more. Help him to know true contentment and to be at
peace with what we have.

*A devout life does bring wealth, but it's the rich simplicity of being yourself
before God. Since we entered the world penniless and will leave it penniless, if
we have bread on the table and shoes on our feet, that's enough. But if it's only
money these leaders are after, they'll self-destruct in no time. Lust for money
brings trouble and nothing but trouble. Going down that path, some lose their
footing in the faith completely and live to regret it bitterly ever after.*

—1 Timothy 6:6–10 MSG

✿ ✿ ✿

(D6) I am concerned for _____. He seems so preoccupied with getting things, and he is afraid he is missing out on what others may have. Please help him respond favorably to all You have given us. Remind him of how You work. You provide for every human concern. May _____ steep his life in Your reality, Your initiative, Your provisions.

What I'm trying to do here is to get you to relax, to not be so preoccupied with getting, so you can respond to God's giving. People who don't know God and the way he works fuss over these things, but you know both God and how he works. Steep your life in God-reality, God-initiative, God-provisions. Don't worry about missing out. You'll find all your everyday human concerns will be met.

—Matthew 6:31–33 MSG

✿ ✿ ✿

(D7) Help _____ live in a way that is honorable and worthy of respect, paying all taxes and all debts. May our debts be kept under control, that all we owe is a huge debt of love to one another.

Fulfill your obligations as a citizen. Pay your taxes, pay your bills, respect your leaders. Don't run up debts, except for the huge debt of love you owe each other. When you love others, you complete what the law has been after all along.

—Romans 13:7–8 MSG

✿ ✿ ✿

(D8)   _____ obeys You, God. He works hard and serves You. As You promise, may his life be filled with pleasantness, joy, and prosperity.

If they obey and serve Him, they shall spend their days in prosperity and their years in pleasantness and joy.

—Job 36:11 AMP

❀ ❀ ❀

(D9)   It is hard when we see people idle away their time, yet get ahead. _____ works so hard. Please bless him with prosperity.

Hard work means prosperity; only fools idle away their time.

—Proverbs 12:11 NLT

E. Health

(E1)   _____ is suffering. He is sick. I earnestly pray to You, God, and will keep on praying in faith that You will heal him and make him well. My sisters and I join together to lift him up in Your name. If _____ has sins that are contributing to his physical sickness, cause him to confess them so he may be healed. I am thankful for my health and sing praises to You for it. I pray for his health, expecting wonderful results.

Are any among you suffering? They should keep on praying about it. And those who have reason to be thankful should continually sing praises to the Lord. Are any among you sick? They should call for the elders of the church and have them pray over them, anointing them with oil in the name of the Lord. And their prayer offered in faith will heal the sick, and the Lord will make them well. And anyone who has committed sins will be forgiven. Confess your sins to each other and pray for each other so that you may be healed. The earnest prayer of a righteous person has great power and wonderful results.

—James 5:13–16 NLT

(E2)   I pray for the health of my beloved _____. May he prosper in every way, that his body and soul will be kept well.

Beloved, I pray that you may prosper in every way and [that your body] may keep well, even as [I know] your soul keeps well and prospers.

—3 John 1:2 AMP

(E3)   Please lay health and healing upon _____. Cure him and reveal to him the abundance of peace and truth.

Behold, [in the future restored Jerusalem] I will lay upon it health and healing, and I will cure them and will reveal to them the abundance of peace (prosperity, security, stability) and truth.

—Jeremiah 33:6 AMP

(E4)   May _____'s eyes be clearly diverted from the things of this world. As he follows Your ways, please restore him to vigorous life and health.

Turn away my eyes from beholding vanity (idols and idolatry); and restore me to vigorous life and health in Your ways.

—Psalm 119:37 AMP

F. Parenting

(F1)   Guide _____ as he manages his family. Gift him with true
        dignity that allows him to keep the children under control.
        May his behaviors command their respect and model re-
        spectfulness to them.

*He must rule his own household well, keeping his children under control,
with true dignity, commanding their respect in every way and keeping them
respectful.*

—1 Timothy 3:4 AMP

❀ ❀ ❀

(F2)   May _____ teach God's commands by how he lives them,
        not just by how he preaches them. May he know Your truth
        so well that he is always ready to use it as an example and
        be able to communicate it to his children in a way they will
        remember even when they are grown. Help us remember
        Your miracles and obey Your commands so we can point
        our children to their hope in You.

*For he issued his decree to Jacob; he gave his law to Israel. He commanded our
ancestors to teach them to their children, so the next generation might know
them—even the children not yet born—that they in turn might teach their
children. So each generation can set its hope anew on God, remembering his
glorious miracles and obeying his commands.*

—Psalm 78:5–7 NLT

❀ ❀ ❀

(F3)   Give wisdom and understanding to _____ that he will
        know just when and how to administer necessary discipline

rather than destroying his family with indulgence. May the children be wise and godly—a source of great joy.

Discipline your children while you still have the chance; indulging them destroys them.

—Proverbs 19:18 MSG

The father of godly children has cause for joy. What a pleasure it is to have wise children.

—Proverbs 23:24 NLT

(F4) Help _____ take the children by the hand and show them what is right rather than coming down hard on them when they are wrong. May we behave in a way that is honorable so they will want to do what we tell them. Help us to guide the children in such a way that they will live well and have a long life.

Children, do what your parents tell you. This is only right. "Honor your father and mother" is the first commandment that has a promise attached to it, namely, "so you will live well and have a long life." Fathers, don't exasperate your children by coming down hard on them. Take them by the hand and lead them in the way of the Master.

—Ephesians 6:1–4 MSG

(F5) Help _____ to keep Your Word inside of him—so that he will be ready and able to impart it to our children. Give him creative ways to teach *Your* truth to them, and help him always to model it before them. Make Your Word a priority in his life.

Write these commandments that I've given you today on your hearts. Get them inside of you and then get them inside your children. Talk about them wherever you are, sitting at home or walking in the street; talk about them from the time you get up in the morning to when you fall into bed at night.
—Deuteronomy 6:6–7 MSG

✿ ✿ ✿

(F6)   Help _____ to discipline in love and not in anger. Help him to be constructive in his corrections so that he will not crush the children's spirits, but will shape them into the godly young people You desire them to be.

Parents, don't come down too hard on your children or you'll crush their spirits.
—Colossians 3:21 MSG

✿ ✿ ✿

(F7)   What a gift You give when You give a husband and wife children! _____ and I long to receive that blessing; we want a "quiver" full. Please give us Your generous legacy.

Don't you see that children are GOD's best gift? The fruit of the womb his generous legacy? Like a warrior's fistful of arrows are the children of a vigorous youth. Oh, how blessed are you parents, with your quivers full of children!
—Psalm 127:3–5 MSG

G. Relationships

(G1)   Help _____ to throw away the worldliness of his former way of life and become a completely new person in You. Allow his coworkers and our friends to see and be opened to this change in him. May _____ be committed to truly putting away the lies and the pretense and replacing those old habits with new ones of integrity and goodness that reflect You, Lord. And give him the boldness never to put up a false front, but always to speak the truth in love to others. Help me to recognize and support this new nature in him.

Throw off your old evil nature and your former way of life, which is rotten through and through, full of lust and deception. Instead, there must be a spiritual renewal of your thoughts and attitudes. You must display a new nature because you are a new person, created in God's likeness—righteous, holy, and true. So put away all falsehood and "tell your neighbor the truth" because we belong to each other.

—Ephesians 4:22–25 NLT

☙ ☙ ☙

(G2)   Help _____ to understand the value of having a partner, whether it's in our marriage or in friendships. Show us as a couple how to share the work and the wealth that comes from it. Teach him to lift up and encourage others when they are down, but not to get discouraged when no one does that for him. Keep us close enough as a couple to warm each other's hearts with love, and help us to realize that with You at the center of our lives, we are a tough bond that's not easily broken.

It's better to have a partner than go it alone. Share the work, share the wealth. And if one falls down, the other helps, but if there's no one to help, tough! Two in a bed warm each other. Alone, you shiver all night. By yourself you're unprotected. With a friend you can face the worst. Can you round up a third? A three-stranded rope isn't easily snapped.

—Ecclesiastes 4:9–12 MSG

❀ ❀ ❀

(G3)   May _____ learn compassion, kindness, and sensitivity
       from Your Word. Help him to realize that others have faults
       and failures, prompting him to forgive more quickly when
       someone offends him. Help him to learn to ask for and
       give forgiveness. Teach him to say "I'm sorry" and mean it,
       by reminding him of the forgiveness You so readily gave
       him. And help me always to respond with forgiveness to-
       ward him as well.

*Since God chose you to be the holy people whom he loves, you must clothe
yourselves with tenderhearted mercy, kindness, humility, gentleness, and patience. You must make allowance for each other's faults and forgive the person
who offends you. Remember, the Lord forgave you, so you must forgive others.*
                                           —Colossians 3:12–13 NLT

❀ ❀ ❀

(G4)   Give _____ true friendships that go beyond the sur-
       face. Guide him on how to be a friend who is faithful, reli-
       able, and trustworthy. Help him to realize that a true friend
       will hold him accountable, even when it hurts to hear the
       truth. While he may have many acquaintances through the
       years, help him to develop some lifelong friends who stick
       by him like family during good and bad times. Make our
       marriage an example of just such an enduring friendship.

You use steel to sharpen steel, and one friend sharpens another.
                                           —Proverbs 27:17 MSG

*Friends love through all kinds of weather, and families stick together in all
kinds of trouble.*
                                           —Proverbs 17:17 MSG

The wounds from a lover are worth it; kisses from an enemy do you in.

—Proverbs 27:6 MSG

Friends come and friends go, but a true friend sticks by you like family.

—Proverbs 18:24 MSG

❀ ❀ ❀

(G5) Help _____ to learn from and speak with respect to older people and to be wise in his advice to the younger ones. Teach him to treat others with the same sensitivity and dignity that he would use with his own parents or family members, whom he adores.

Never speak harshly to an older man, but appeal to him respectfully as though he were your own father. Talk to the younger men as you would to your own brothers. Treat the older women as you would your mother, and treat the younger women with all purity as your own sisters.

—1 Timothy 5:1–2 NLT

❀ ❀ ❀

(G6) May _____ this day gain wisdom directly from You and then display those good deeds so that others may see You in him. Help him never to be jealous of others' success, nor to brag about his own. Remind him that selfish ambition will bring only false prosperity that will leave him empty, incomplete, and in disarray. Show _____ that he will find true fulfillment when he seeks Your ways and then responds with fairness, good judgment, and kindness. Teach him to take on the role of peacemaker, and reward him for his efforts. Help me to offer words of encouragement so that together we would serve others with a gentle heart.

If you are wise and understand God's ways, live a life of steady goodness so that only good deeds will pour forth. And if you don't brag about the good you do, then you will be truly wise! But if you are bitterly jealous and there is selfish ambition in your hearts, don't brag about being wise. That is the worst kind of lie. For jealousy and selfishness are not God's kind of wisdom. Such things are earthly, unspiritual, and motivated by the Devil. For wherever there is jealousy and selfish ambition, there you will find disorder and every kind of evil. But the wisdom that comes from heaven is first of all pure. It is also peace loving, gentle at all times, and willing to yield to others. It is full of mercy and good deeds. It shows no partiality and is always sincere. And those who are peacemakers will plant seeds of peace and reap a harvest of goodness.

—James 3:13–18 NLT

H. Sex

(H1)   Cover us with Your blessings as we keep our bed a sacred retreat. May _____ know in his heart that he is the only one for me and that he fulfills me like no other could, for he is the one You gave to me. Guard him from the temptation of lust, adultery, pornography, or immoral behavior that could jeopardize the purity of our intimacy. Help me to be the wife that he needs, and increase our love for each other daily.

Honor marriage, and guard the sacredness of sexual intimacy between wife and husband. God draws a firm line against casual and illicit sex.

—Hebrews 13:4 MSG

✿ ✿ ✿

(H2)   Please help _____ always to be satisfied with our love. When temptation comes his way, help him to turn away and remain faithful always to me, as me to him. Help me to be attentive to his needs so that he will have no need to look elsewhere. Keep my mind and body attractive to him so he can rejoice in me. Help me to relax and enjoy my time with _____. Show us new ways to enhance and have fun with each other so we are not tempted to look elsewhere for pleasure. Make us as content with each other as we were when our love was young and new, but even more satisfied in our marriage as each year bonds us closer together in love, companionship, and friendship.

Drink water from your own well—share your love only with your wife. Why spill the water of your springs in public, having sex with just anyone? You should reserve it for yourselves. Don't share it with strangers. Let your wife be a fountain of blessing for you. Rejoice in the wife of your youth. She is a loving doe, a graceful deer. Let her breasts satisfy you always. May you always be captivated by her love. Why be captivated, my son, with an immoral woman, or embrace the breasts of an adulterous woman?
—Proverbs 5:15–20 NLT

❋ ❋ ❋

(H3)   May _____ always see me as his "beloved," and may his desire always be for me and me alone. Help us to be sensitive to each other's needs and to find great satisfaction in our union together.

I am my lover's. I'm all he wants. I'm all the world to him!
—Song of Songs 7:10 MSG

I. Spiritual Life

(I1)   Let _____ not focus on the things of this world. Keep him from the temptation to do things the way others do in trying to get ahead in life. Instead, Lord, help _____ to think about how You would expect him to live and work. May he submit himself to You daily, allowing Your Holy Spirit to control his thoughts and actions, so that all he does is pleasing to You.

Those who are dominated by the sinful nature think about sinful things, but those who are controlled by the Holy Spirit think about things that please the Spirit.

—Romans 8:5 NLT

✿ ✿ ✿

(I2)   May _____ realize how blessed he is because of You. Give him a passion to become a better man with each passing day. Add to his faith a deeper understanding of how You want him to live and act. Help him to cooperate with You as You teach him self-control, develop his endurance, and mature his faith in You. Show him how to become a man of strong character. Give him confidence to make better choices. Bless him as he matures into a positive role model for our family and others.

So don't lose a minute in building on what you've been given, complementing your basic faith with good character, spiritual understanding, alert discipline, passionate patience, reverent wonder, warm friendliness, and generous love, each dimension fitting into and developing the others. With these qualities active and growing in your lives, no grass will grow under your feet, no day will pass without its reward as you mature in your experience of our Master Jesus.

—2 Peter 1:5–8 MSG

✿ ✿ ✿

(13)   Open _____'s eyes to the emptiness of the things that this world offers. Show him the futility of striving for things that do not last and offer only temporary satisfaction. Keep him from becoming selfish, self-indulgent, or self-important, because that's completely opposite from You, Lord. Help him to see the true and lasting effects of doing things Your way, and to realize the amazing benefits of doing things Your way for now and eternity.

Don't love the world's ways. Don't love the world's goods. Love of the world squeezes out love for the Father. Practically everything that goes on in the world—wanting your own way, wanting everything for yourself, wanting to appear important—has nothing to do with the Father. It just isolates you from him. The world and all its wanting, wanting, wanting is on the way out—but whoever does what God wants is set for eternity.

—1 John 2:15–17 MSG

✿ ✿ ✿

(14)   Help _____ to live, work, and walk in a manner that is pleasing to You. Help all that he does bring honor to You, God. And as he gets to know You better, help him apply what he is learning to the way he is living.

Then the way you live will always honor and please the Lord, and you will continually do good, kind things for others. All the while, you will learn to know God better and better.

—Colossians 1:10 NLT

✿ ✿ ✿

(I5)   Please reward _____ for doing the right thing. Help his
         motives to be pure. Show him the distinct and definite ad-
         vantages to being faithful, honest, and committed to You.
         Stand up for him when others try to do him wrong.

> The LORD rewarded me for doing right, because of the innocence of my hands
> in his sight. To the faithful you show yourself faithful; to those with integrity
> you show integrity. To the pure you show yourself pure, but to the wicked you
> show yourself hostile.
> —Psalm 18:24–26 NLT

> The LORD himself will fight for you. You won't have to lift a finger in your
> defense!
> —Exodus 14:14 NLT

❁ ❁ ❁

(I6)   May _____ always recognize the good counsel and
         protection of Your Word. May he be hungry for Your in-
         sight and guidance. Help him to forsake his prideful, re-
         bellious ways and always desire to obey Your teachings,
         for You never fail to fulfill Your promises.

> Help me abandon my shameful ways; your laws are all I want in life. I long
> to obey your commandments! Renew my life with your goodness. LORD, give
> to me your unfailing love, the salvation that you promised me.
> —Psalm 119:39–41 NLT

❁ ❁ ❁

(I7)   Grant Your peace to _____ in all areas of his life,
         especially during difficult days and troubling times. Help
         him to feel the comfort of Your presence no matter what
         comes his way.

Now may the Lord of peace Himself grant you His peace (the peace of His kingdom) at all times and in all ways [under all circumstances and conditions, whatever comes]. The Lord [be] with you all.

—2 Thessalonians 3:16 AMP

❦ ❦ ❦

(I8)   Sometimes _____ wants to figure out everything on his own. He can at times tend to assume he knows it all. Help _____ to trust You—from the bottom of his heart— with his life and all its details. May he listen for Your voice in everything he does and everywhere he goes. Please keep him on track—running from evil and running to You!

Trust GOD from the bottom of your heart; don't try to figure out everything on your own. Listen for GOD's voice in everything you do, everywhere you go; he's the one who will keep you on track. Don't assume that you know it all. Run to GOD! Run from evil!

—Proverbs 3:5–7 MSG

J. Trials

(J1)   Help _____ to understand that, yes, trials will come, but that he will never face them alone. Let him see the positive that can come from taking on these challenges. Give him the strength to tackle the problem. Then build his confidence as he progresses. After _____ has survived this test, give him renewed strength to take on the next one, knowing that with You he will not fail.

Dear brothers and sisters, whenever trouble comes your way, let it be an opportunity for joy. For when your faith is tested, your endurance has a chance

*to grow. So let it grow, for when your endurance is fully developed, you will
be strong in character and ready for anything.*

—James 1:2–4 NLT

(J2)   When times are tough and _____ feels surrounded by
        enemies, let him fall back into Your arms for protection,
        comfort, and guidance. Show him that You will take over
        and fight the battle for him, with inevitable victory.

*The eternal God is your refuge, and his everlasting arms are under you. He
thrusts out the enemy before you; it is he who cries, "Destroy them!"*

—Deuteronomy 33:27 NLT

❀ ❀ ❀

(J3)   May _____ never forget that today, tomorrow, and
        even when he is old, You will take care of him—that he is
        never alone or abandoned. You will carry him along and
        save him.

*I will be your God throughout your lifetime—until your hair is white with
age. I made you, and I will care for you. I will carry you along and save
you.*

—Isaiah 46:4 NLT

❀ ❀ ❀

(J4)   I'm desperately pleading for Your help for _____ during
        this overwhelming hardship in his life. May the shadow of
        Your wings protect him during this violent storm. Rescue

him from those who are out to get him. Remind us of Your faithfulness and Your fulfilled promises to us in the past.

Have mercy on me, O God, have mercy! I look to you for protection. I will hide beneath the shadow of your wings until this violent storm is past. I cry out to God Most High, to God who will fulfill his purpose for me. He will send help from heaven to save me, rescuing me from those who are out to get me. My God will send forth his unfailing love and faithfulness.

—Psalm 57:1–3 NLT

(J5)   Life's a struggle. At times it hurts, and _____ falls down. Help _____ remember that You can lift him up again and give him the strength to keep on going. Even when he is confused about why this is happening to him, remind him that he's not alone, he's not forgotten, and he's not abandoned. As _____ knows that You raised Jesus from the dead, You will also raise him above any circumstance that he encounters. May this knowledge help him get up and keep on going.

We are pressed on every side by troubles, but we are not crushed and broken. We are perplexed, but we don't give up and quit. We are hunted down, but God never abandons us. We get knocked down, but we get up again and keep going.

—2 Corinthians 4:8–9 NLT

We know that the same God who raised our Lord Jesus will also raise us with Jesus and present us to himself along with you.

—2 Corinthians 4:14 NLT

❀ ❀ ❀

(J6)   May _____ always be passionate about serving You,
        in fulfilling whatever assignment You give him. Keep him
        cheerful as he works, knowing that in pleasing You he will
        be rewarded. Give him boundless energy to do each task,
        no matter how hard. And when things get tough, remind
        him to pray for the strength to keep going. We never want
        to forget the importance of diligent prayer.

Don't burn out; keep yourselves fueled and aflame. Be alert servants of the
Master, cheerfully expectant. Don't quit in hard times; pray all the harder.
                                           —Romans 12:11–12 MSG

K. Unity

(K1)   Help _____ to love like Christ. May he not hold back
        in his love for me; instead help him give it all he has, not
        expecting to get anything in return. Let me respond by
        showing that same kind of love to him, not cautious, but
        extravagant.

Mostly what God does is love you. Keep company with him and learn a life
of love. Observe how Christ loved us. His love was not cautious but extrava-
gant. He didn't love in order to get something from us but to give everything of
himself to us. Love like that.
                                           —Ephesians 5:2 MSG

❀ ❀ ❀

(K2)   Help _____ and me always to be deep-spirited friends,
        soul mates, and lovers, always being more considerate of

each other than ourselves. Teach us how to agree more and argue less. May we support and encourage each other, never letting one push ahead and leave the other behind. Keep us from becoming selfish and trying to get our own way.

Then do me a favor: Agree with each other, love each other, be deep-spirited friends. Don't push your way to the front; don't sweet-talk your way to the top. Put yourself aside, and help others get ahead. Don't be obsessed with getting your own advantage. Forget yourselves long enough to lend a helping hand.

—Philippians 2:2–4 MSG

✿ ✿ ✿

(K3)   Keep _____ and me always walking in harmony with each other in our hearts. Don't let us become too independent of each other and so busy doing our own thing that we forget to do for each other. Help us to always express our praise and thankfulness for all You've done for us.

Let the peace of Christ keep you in tune with each other, in step with each other. None of this going off and doing your own thing. And cultivate thankfulness.

—Colossians 3:15 MSG

✿ ✿ ✿

(K4)   You have made it so clear, Lord, that You want us to get along. I plead with You to help us not to argue with each other or with other people. Teach us how to stand united in thought and deed. Stop us from tearing apart what we've worked hard to build. Help us to be single minded in all that we do.

Now, dear brothers and sisters, I appeal to you by the authority of the Lord Jesus Christ to stop arguing among yourselves. Let there be real harmony so there won't be divisions in the church. I plead with you to be of one mind, united in thought and purpose.

—1 Corinthians 1:10 NLT

✿ ✿ ✿

(K5)   Patience and encouragement are gifts from You, God. May we use these attributes to live together in harmony. Help _____ and me to treat each other the way that Jesus treated others, with love, kindness, and goodness. If we learn to live together in that kind of harmony, it will help us to get along with others, too. Help us to realize that the better we treat each other as Christians, the better example we set for the world, bringing honor to You, our Father and Lord.

May God, who gives this patience and encouragement, help you live in complete harmony with each other—each with the attitude of Christ Jesus toward the other. Then all of you can join together with one voice, giving praise and glory to God, the Father of our Lord Jesus Christ.

—Romans 15:5–6 NLT

✿ ✿ ✿

(K6)   May _____ realize that as followers of Jesus, we have the Holy Spirit within as a helper. Help him every day to listen to the Holy Spirit's voice for direction. Don't let the loudness of the world drown out the quietness of Your truth. Keep _____ from becoming conceited or self-important. Don't let him be an irritant to others. Stop jealousy from creeping into his heart. Help him be satisfied with the blessings that come from You.

If we are living now by the Holy Spirit, let us follow the Holy Spirit's leading in every part of our lives. Let us not become conceited, or irritate one another, or be jealous of one another.

—Galatians 5:25–26 NLT

❦ ❦ ❦

(K7)   Help me to be the wife that _____ needs me to be. Guide me so that my behavior is gentle, gracious, and pure. May _____ see You in me and want to be a follower of You. Show me how to focus not on how I look, but on how I act. Let _____ see a beauty in me that comes from You. Direct his thoughts and actions so that he always treats me well. Help him to honor and appreciate my place in his life. Make us true companions.

The same goes for you wives: Be good wives to your husbands, responsive to their needs. There are husbands who, indifferent as they are to any words about God, will be captivated by your life of holy beauty. What matters is not your outer appearance—the styling of your hair, the jewelry you wear, the cut of your clothes—but your inner disposition. Cultivate inner beauty, the gentle, gracious kind that God delights in. . . . The same goes for you husbands: Be good husbands to your wives. Honor them, delight in them. As women they lack some of your advantages. But in the new life of God's grace, you're equals. Treat your wives, then, as equals so your prayers don't run aground.

—1 Peter 3:1–4, 7 MSG

❦ ❦ ❦

(K8)   Bless _____ and me with one heart, one mind, so that all that we have may be shared with each other.

All the believers were of one heart and mind, and they felt that what they
owned was not their own; they shared everything they had.

—Acts 4:32 NLT

L. Work

(L1)   Help _____ be his very best—good, right, and true.
May he do his work in a spirit of prayerful worship and as
a result be a success.

Hezekiah carried out this work and kept it up everywhere in Judah. He was
the very best—good, right, and true before his GOD. Everything he took up,
whether it had to do with worship in God's Temple or the carrying out of God's
Law and Commandments, he did well in a spirit of prayerful worship. He was
a great success.

—2 Chronicles 31:20–21 MSG

❀ ❀ ❀

(L2)   Help _____ to make the most of his job and to truly enjoy his work as a God-given gift. May he accept Your gift
and delight in the work. Thank You for the bounty You
provide and for the capacity to enjoy it.

After looking at the way things are on this earth, here's what I've decided is the
best way to live: Take care of yourself, have a good time, and make the most of
whatever job you have for as long as God gives you life. And that's about it.
That's the human lot. Yes, we should make the most of what God gives, both
the bounty and the capacity to enjoy it, accepting what's given and delighting
in the work. It's God's gift!

—Ecclesiastes 5:18–19 MSG

(L3)   Bless _____ as he works hard each day. Give him the strength to complete each week. Help him to know that at the end of the week, he can feel good because he does not just talk, but he works hard.

Hard work always pays off; mere talk puts no bread on the table.
                                    —Proverbs 14:23 MSG

(L4)   I pray that _____ will have the strength to stick it out over the long haul at work—not from the grim, teeth-gritting strength that comes from his own ability, but from the glorious power that comes from You alone. Give me encouraging words for him at the end of each day. Give him the kind of strength that produces patience and endurance that spills over into joy in the end.

We pray that you'll have the strength to stick it out over the long haul—not the grim strength of gritting your teeth but the glory-strength God gives. It is strength that endures the unendurable and spills over into joy.
                                    —Colossians 1:11 MSG

(L5)   May _____ be like Christ in his work, not pushing his way to the front, but putting himself aside to help others get ahead. As _____ takes on the attributes of Christ—with the same attitude, purpose, and mind—may he become one with You. Likewise, show me how to prefer him in honor and be considerate enough of him to set aside my schedule, my job, and my wants to listen to his needs and help him meet them.

Don't push your way to the front; don't sweet-talk your way to the top. Put yourself aside, and help others get ahead. Don't be obsessed with getting your own advantage. Forget yourselves long enough to lend a helping hand. Think of yourselves the way Christ Jesus thought of himself. He had equal status with God but didn't think so much of himself that he had to cling to the advantages of that status no matter what.
—Philippians 2:3–6 MSG

(L6)   Help _____ be strong and courageous in the face of the world's standards that conflict with what he knows to be true. May he be on guard and stand true to what he believes.

Be on guard. Stand true to what you believe. Be courageous. Be strong.
—1 Corinthians 16:13 NLT

(L7)   Help _____ to be a man of true honesty and integrity before You. Remind him of the admonitions in Your Word and how You advise him to be fair and execute right principles in dealing with those in his work environment. Help me to be encouraging to him as he shares with me his struggles and challenges, and to pray with him concerning his desires and needs.

The LORD demands fairness in every business deal; he sets the standard.
—Proverbs 16:11 NLT

(L8)   Though it may be hard for _____ to remain honest
       when dishonest people seem to get ahead, help him to be
       guided by honesty and not dishonesty, which destroys those
       who choose to use treacherous tactics.

*Good people are guided by their honesty; treacherous people are destroyed by
their dishonesty.*

—Proverbs 11:3 NLT

❀ ❀ ❀

(L9)   Allow _____ the insight to learn from others—observing
       those who are good at their work and listening to wise
       counsel. Help me to lend an eager ear to what he has learned
       and share his input with enthusiasm.

*Refuse good advice and watch your plans fail; take good counsel and watch
them succeed.*

—Proverbs 15:22 MSG

*Observe people who are good at their work—skilled workers are always in
demand and admired; they don't take a back seat to anyone.*

—Proverbs 22:29 MSG

❀ ❀ ❀

(L10) Help _____ to be obedient to his earthly boss, always
       doing his best whether his supervisor is watching or not,
       realizing that You are his true boss and You are always
       watching. And because he is really serving You, help him

to remember that his real reward will come from You. Keep
_____ from being a reluctant or deceptive worker, knowing that You will hold each person responsible for his or
her own efforts and that his coworkers are watching him as
a Christian.

*Servants, do what you're told by your earthly masters. And don't just do the
minimum that will get you by. Do your best. Work from the heart for your
real Master, for God, confident that you'll get paid in full when you come into
your inheritance. Keep in mind always that the ultimate Master you're serving is Christ. The sullen servant who does shoddy work will be held responsible. Being Christian doesn't cover up bad work.*
—Colossians 3:22–25 MSG

❦ ❦ ❦

(L11)   _____ is diligent and skillful in his work. May he always be in demand and admired.

*Observe people who are good at their work—skilled workers are always in
demand and admired; they don't take a back seat to anyone.*
—Proverbs 22:29 MSG

*Do you see a man diligent and skillful in his business? He will stand before
kings; he will not stand before obscure men.*
—Proverbs 22:29 AMP

❦ ❦ ❦

(L12)   _____ is a smart man, but please keep him from being
impressed with his own wisdom and depending on his own
understanding. Instead, help him to trust You with all his
heart, to seek Your will in all he does, to fear You and turn

his back on evil. Please direct his path so he will honor You with his wealth. Fill him with loyalty and kindness that he may find favor with You and with man. Grant him a good reputation. Give him renewed health and vitality so that he may be blessed with success.

Never let loyalty and kindness get away from you! Wear them like a necklace; write them deep within your heart. Then you will find favor with both God and people, and you will gain a good reputation. Trust in the LORD with all your heart; do not depend on your own understanding. Seek his will in all you do, and he will direct your paths. Don't be impressed with your own wisdom. Instead, fear the LORD and turn your back on evil. Then you will gain renewed health and vitality. Honor the LORD with your wealth and with the best part of everything your land produces. Then he will fill your barns with grain, and your vats will overflow with the finest wine.

—Proverbs 3:3–10 NLT

❀ ❀ ❀

(L13)   As a leader in his company, _____ is followed every day by the employees under him. He establishes the mood for the company, and sets the pace at which work is done. Let him always set a pace that is reasonable and create a mood that is pleasing to You. Give _____ real understanding in every situation so that he can straighten out any problem that arises. As he does his job from day to day, guide him in his decisions. Be his ample refuge when he needs a break.

I was their leader, establishing the mood and setting the pace by which they lived. Where I led, they followed.

—Job 29:25 MSG

GOD is all strength for his people, ample refuge for his chosen leader.

—Psalm 28:8 MSG

When the country is in chaos, everybody has a plan to fix it—but it takes a leader of real understanding to straighten things out.

—Proverbs 28:2 MSG

Appendix B

Prayer Request Form

Date: _____

Prayer Request for: _____
_____
_____

Answered? _____

Date answered: _____

Date: _____

Prayer Request for: _____
_____
_____

Answered? _____

Date answered: _____

Date: _____

Prayer Request for: _____

_____

_____

Answered? _____

Date answered: _____

Date: _____

Prayer Request for: _____

_____

_____

Answered? _____

Date answered: _____

Date: _____

Prayer Request for: _____

_____

_____

Answered? _____

Date answered: _____

Date: _____

Prayer Request for: _____

_____

_____

Answered? _____

Date answered: _____

_____

Date: _____

Prayer Request for: _____

_____

_____

Answered? _____

Date answered: _____

_____

Date: _____

Prayer Request for: _____

_____

_____

Answered? _____

Date answered: _____

Date: _____

Prayer Request for: _____
_____
_____

Answered? _____

Date answered: _____

Date: _____

Prayer Request for: _____
_____
_____

Answered? _____

Date answered: _____

Date: _____

Prayer Request for: _____
_____
_____

Answered? _____

Date answered: _____

Appendix C

Personality Overviews

Popular Sanguine
"Let's do it the fun way"

Desire: to have fun

Emotional needs: attention, affection, approval, acceptance

Key strengths: ability to talk about anything at any time at any place, bubbling personality, optimism, sense of humor, storytelling ability, enjoyment of people

Key weaknesses: disorganized, can't remember details or names, exaggerates, not serious about anything, trusts others to do the work, too gullible and naive

Get depressed when: life is no fun and no one seems to love them

Are afraid of: being unpopular or bored, having to live by the clock, having to keep a record of money spent

Like people who: listen and laugh, praise and approve

Dislike people who: criticize, don't respond to their humor, don't think they're cute

Are valuable in work for: colorful creativity, optimism, light touch, cheering up others, entertaining

Could improve if they: got organized, didn't talk so much, learned
    to tell time
As leaders they: excite, persuade, and inspire others; exude charm
    and entertain; are forgetful and poor on follow-through
Tend to marry: Perfect Melancholies, who are sensitive and seri-
    ous, but they quickly tire of having to cheer them up, and they
    soon tire of being made to feel inadequate or stupid
Reaction to stress: leave the scene, go shopping, find a fun group,
    create excuses, blame others
Recognized by their: constant talking, loud volume, bright eyes

Powerful Choleric
"Let's do it my way"

Desire: to have control
Emotional needs: sense of obedience, appreciation for accomplish-
    ments, credit for ability
Key strengths: ability to take charge of anything instantly and to
    make quick, correct judgments
Key weaknesses: too bossy, domineering, autocratic, insensitive,
    impatient, unwilling to delegate or give credit to others
Get depressed when: life is out of control and people won't do
    things their way
Are afraid of: losing control of anything (e.g., losing a job, not
    being promoted, becoming seriously ill, having a rebellious
    child or unsupportive mate)
Like people who: are supportive and submissive, see things their
    way, cooperate quickly, let them take credit
Dislike people who: are lazy and not interested in working con-
    stantly, buck their authority, become independent, aren't loyal

Are valuable in work because they: can accomplish more than anyone else in a shorter time, are usually right

Could improve if they: allowed others to make decisions, delegated authority, became more patient, didn't expect everyone to produce as they do

As leaders they have: a natural feel for being in charge, a quick sense of what will work, a sincere belief in their ability to achieve, a potential to overwhelm less aggressive people

Tend to marry: Peaceful Phlegmatics, who will quietly obey and not buck their authority, but who never accomplish enough or get excited over their projects

Reaction to stress: tighten control, work harder, exercise more, get rid of the offender

Recognized by their: fast-moving approach, quick grab for control, self-confidence, restless and overpowering attitude

Perfect Melancholies
"Let's do it the right way"

Desire: to have it right

Emotional needs: sense of stability, space, silence, sensitivity, support

Key strengths: ability to organize and set long-range goals, have high standards and ideals, analyze deeply

Key weaknesses: easily depressed, too much time on preparation, too focused on details, remember negatives, suspicious of others

Get depressed when: life is out of order, standards aren't met, and no one seems to care

Are afraid of: no one understanding how they really feel, making a mistake, having to compromise standards

Like people who: are serious, intellectual, deep, and will carry on a sensible conversation

Dislike people who: are lightweights, forgetful, late, disorganized, superficial, prevaricating, and unpredictable

Are valuable in work for: sense of detail, love of analysis, follow-through, high standards of performance, compassion for the hurting

Could improve if they: didn't take life quite so seriously, didn't insist others be perfectionists

As leaders they: organize well, are sensitive to people's feelings, have deep creativity, want quality performance

Tend to marry: Popular Sanguines for their outgoing personality and social skills, but whom they soon attempt to quiet and get on a schedule

Reaction to stress: withdraw, get lost in a book, become depressed, give up, recount the problems

Recognized by their: serious and sensitive nature, well-mannered approach, self-deprecating comments, meticulous and well-groomed looks

Peaceful Phlegmatic
"Let's do it the easy way"

Desire: to avoid conflict, keep peace

Emotional needs: sense of respect, feeling of worth, understanding, emotional support

Key strengths: balance, even disposition, dry sense of humor, pleasing personality

Key weaknesses: lack of decisiveness, enthusiasm, and energy; a hidden will of iron

Get depressed when: life is full of conflict, they have to face a personal confrontation, no one wants to help, the buck stops with them

Are afraid of: having to deal with a major personal problem, being left holding the bag, making major changes

Like people who: will make decisions for them, will recognize their strengths, will not ignore them, will give them respect

Dislike people who: are too pushy, too loud, and expect too much of them

Are valuable in work because they: mediate between contentious people, objectively solve problems

Could improve if they: set goals and became self-motivated, were willing to do more and move faster than expected, could face their own problems as well as they handle those of others

As leaders they: keep calm, cool, and collected; don't make impulsive decisions; are well liked and inoffensive; won't cause trouble; don't often come up with brilliant new ideas

Tend to marry: Powerful Cholerics who are strong and decisive, but they soon tire of being pushed around and looked down upon

Reaction to stress: hide from it, watch TV, eat, tune out life

Recognized by their: calm approach, relaxed posture (sitting or leaning when possible)

For additional information on the personalities, read *Personality Puzzle* by Florence Littauer and Marita Littauer (Grand Rapids: Revell, 1992); *Your Spiritual Personality: Using the Strengths of Your Personality to Deepen Your Relationship with God* by Marita Littauer with Betty Southard (San Francisco: Jossey-Bass, 2005); and *Wired That Way* by Marita Littauer (Ventura, Calif.: Regal, May 2006). They are all available through your favorite booksellers.

About the Authors

Marita Littauer

Marita Littauer has been speaking professionally for more than twenty-five years for church, school, and business groups. She is the author of sixteen books, including *But Lord, I Was Happy Shallow; Your Spiritual Personality; The Journey to Jesus; Making the Blue Plate Special;* and *Wired That Way.*

Based on Romans 12:18, Marita is known through her personal speaking ministry for her expertise in personal and professional relationships. She uses the entertaining and educational concepts that have become universally known as "The Personalities." This teaching is the foundation for, or included in, many of her books.

Marita is the president of CLASServices Inc., an organization that provides resources, training, and promotion for Christian speakers and authors. Through the CLASSeminar, which has been offered throughout the United States since 1981, Marita has trained thousands of men and women in speaking and writing skills. Many of the concepts presented at the CLASSeminar can be found in her book *Communication Plus.*

Marita is a columnist for the *Godly Business Woman Magazine* and CBN.com, and a regular contributor to *The Christian Communicator Magazine* and *Writers Digest*. She is a member of the National Speakers Association and is a frequent guest on TV and radio programs throughout the country.

On a personal note, Marita and her husband, Chuck Noon, have been married since 1983 and have two schnauzers. Chuck is a licensed professional clinical counselor specializing in marriage. They live in Albuquerque, New Mexico.

Dianne Anderson

An award winning journalist, Dianne was honored with the "Best of the Best" award from the National Association of Broadcasters in 1997. More recently, she received the "Media Award" from the National Foundation for Women Legislators in 2002.

She and her husband, Mark Mathis, are currently the hosts of a midday radio talk show on 106.3 Talk FM. KAGM is the first commercial FM talk radio station in Albuquerque. Before this new venture, she served as a news anchor for New Mexico's ABC Affiliate KOAT for fifteen years.

Dianne is well-known throughout New Mexico. She frequently emcees charitable and civic functions within the state and speaks to women's church and business groups. *The Praying Wives Club* is her first book.

Along with his cohost duties on Talk FM, her husband, Mark, is a former KOAT news reporter who now works as a media consultant and trainer. They enjoy teaching premarital classes at their church. They have two children, Weston and Waverly, and live in Albuquerque, New Mexico.

Permissions

But Lord, I Was Happy Shallow
Lessons Learned in the Deep Places
By Marita Littauer
0-8254-3160-3

"Real people dealing with real issues—how refreshing! This book is for any woman who wants to get out from under her circumstances, walk *through* the valley, and up on to the mountain of hope, faith, and joy."

—PAM FARREL

Author of best-selling *Men Are Like Waffles, Women Are Like Spaghetti, Woman of Influence,* and *10 Best Decisions a Woman Can Make*

Don't Miss!

Tailor-Made Marriage
When Your Lives Aren't One Size Fits All
By Marita Littauer and Chuck Noon
0-8254-3161-1

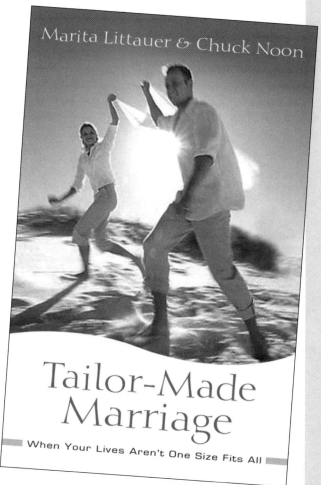

"We read daily about world conflicts, but the ones that impact us most profoundly are the ones in our living rooms. Marita and Chuck—in practical and personal ways—help us face our reactions to today's pressures on our marriages. This book is packed with love!"
   —PATSY CLAIRMONT
   Women of Faith speaker and author of *Mending Your Heart in a Broken World*